# The Wheat-Free Meat-Free Cookbook

## 100 Gluten-Free Vegetarian Recipes

Kalinda Piper

## Disclaimer

The author is not a medical professional. Neither the author nor the publisher makes any warranty as to the suitability of this book for any particular purpose nor as to the suitability of the recipes contained within for any particular individual. If you have any doubts whatsoever about whether you can safely eat a particular food, please speak with your medical professional.

# Dedication

Mom and Dad, who sparked a life-long interest in food. You showed me that cooking is essential, but creating a meal for others is truly a delight.

Lissa and Braden, forever relegated to washing mushrooms and stirring sauce with me. Your criticisms and encouragement have been invaluable during this process.

Mike, this book wouldn't exist without you. There aren't enough words to say thanks.

# Your Feedback is Appreciated!

As the author of this book, I'm very interested to hear your thoughts. If you find the book helpful, please let me know! Alternatively, if you have any suggestions of ways to make the book better, I'm eager to hear that, too.

Finally, if you're unsatisfied with your purchase for any reason, let me know, and I'll be happy to provide you with a refund of the current list price of the book (limited to one refund per household).

You can reach me at: kalinda@wheatfreemeatfree.com.

Best Regards,
Kalinda

# Table of Contents

## Soups and a Bread

## Sides

# Mains

# Desserts

# Introduction and Notes

Before we get down to business, I want to share a little background on who I am and how my family eats. I have also included some general assumptions that I used when writing this cookbook, so that we can be on the same page when it comes to successfully executing the recipes.

I started writing wheatfreemeatfree.com, and have now written this cookbook, because my husband, Mike, requires a gluten-free diet and he happens to be vegetarian.

Mike is technically a lacto-ovo vegetarian, meaning he eats dairy and eggs. As a result, there are recipes that include one, or the other, or both. I'll also note that he does not worry about whether cheese is made with animal rennet. Most cheeses can be found in vegetarian-friendly varieties. Please seek those out if this is important to you.

Fortunately, Mike does not have other food allergies or intolerances that frequently go hand-in-hand with Celiac disease/gluten sensitivity. As a result, there are many recipes that include other common allergens like nuts or soy. One thing you'll note is that any recipes that require milk list soymilk. This is simply because soymilk is what our family drinks (rather than dairy milk or other non-dairy alternatives). While I cannot guarantee that other milks will work in all the recipes, in many cases such substitutions should be fine.

Since this is a gluten-free cookbook, I'm assuming you're using gluten-free ingredients. I have tried to specify "gluten-free" for ingredients that are more common in gluten-full versions and for ingredients where it might not be obvious that they can contain gluten, but please keep in mind that you need to check to make sure all of your ingredients are gluten-free.

I encourage everyone to follow one of the golden rules of cooking, which is to taste as you go and make adjustments if necessary. Most importantly, this refers to salt. Salt is a special ingredient in that it enhances the other flavors in a dish. The goal is not to a make a dish taste salty, but to bring forward the other flavors. I do not specify amounts of salt in many of my recipes. When I cook, I'll add a pinch of salt, then taste the dish. I'll do this multiple times throughout the cooking process, and I would encourage you to do the same.

While salt is the main spice to be concerned with, tasting as you go applies to all herbs and spices. I have tried darned hard to make tasty dishes, but that doesn't mean my palate necessarily matches yours. If you like a lot of heat, you may try a dish and decide it needs more cayenne. Or maybe you're a citrus nut and decide you want to add extra lemon zest to a dish. No recipe is set in stone. Taste throughout the cooking process and make adjustments. You're the one who is going to eat this food, after all.

One of the other golden rules of cooking that I'll encourage you to follow is to read the recipe all the way through before you begin. You'll get an idea of how long a recipe will take. (Does something need to be prepped hours in advance?) You'll also know what ingredients and tools to have out and ready before you begin. Not having the right tool or ingredient ready when you need it can be a good way to mess up a dish.

With regards to baking, I measure flour by spooning it into the measuring cup, then leveling it off. This is done to help keep the measurements consistent. If you measure by scooping the flour out of a container with the measuring cup, you could end up with much more flour packed into the cup, which will throw the recipe off. I mostly use Bob's Red Mill flours, since they are widely available.

And now, it's time for the recipes...

# Breakfasts

# Glazed Doughnuts

## Doughnuts
2 tablespoons white sugar
¾ cup warm unsweetened soymilk
2 teaspoons active dry yeast
¾ cup tapioca starch
¾ cup white rice flour
¼ cup sorghum flour
¼ cup millet flour
1 teaspoon xanthan gum
½ teaspoon salt
1 large egg, room temperature
2 tablespoons butter, melted
½ teaspoon vanilla extract
peanut or vegetable oil for frying

## Glaze
2½ cups powdered sugar
¼ cup unsweetened soymilk
¼ teaspoon vanilla extract

1. In a small bowl, stir the sugar into the warm milk until dissolved. Add the yeast and let sit until bubbly.
2. Thoroughly whisk the starch, flours, xanthan gum, and salt in a medium bowl.
3. Put the egg in the bowl of a stand mixer and beat until fluffy. Add the butter, vanilla, and yeasted milk and mix until combined. Add the flours and mix on medium

speed, making sure to scrape down the sides, until the dough comes together. Do not over mix.

4. Form the dough into a ball shape. Cover the bowl with a damp towel, and set in a warm space for 30 minutes. Dough should rise slightly.

5. Turn the dough out onto a well-floured surface; it will be wet and sticky. Sprinkle liberally with additional flour, and using a light touch, roll the dough out to just under ½-inch thickness. Cut using a 3½-inch doughnut cutter.*** Carefully move cut doughnuts to a floured surface. Reform the remaining dough into a ball, roll out again, and cut another batch of doughnuts. Continue rolling and cutting until all the dough has been used. Remaining dough scraps can be rolled into small balls for doughnut holes.

6. Cover the doughnuts with a lightweight towel, and let sit for 60 minutes. They should become puffy.

7. For the glaze, whisk the powdered sugar, milk, and vanilla in a small pot. Set over medium-low heat, whisk until the sugar dissolves, then reduce heat to low to keep warm and prevent the glaze from solidifying.

8. Add a few inches of oil to the bottom of a medium to large pot. Set over high heat. Once the oil reaches 375°F, add a few doughnuts, taking care not to overcrowd the pot. Cook until starting to brown around the edges, 45-60 seconds. Flip the doughnuts and cook another 45-60 seconds. Remove and set on paper towels to absorb extra oil. Make sure the oil comes back to 375°F

before adding the next set of doughnuts. Continue until all of the doughnuts have been fried.

9. Once the doughnuts have cooled slightly, dip in the glaze to coat both sides, then set on cooling racks placed over a baking sheet to catch drips.

Makes 8 doughnuts + holes

***If you don't have a doughnut cutter, use a similarly sized tumbler glass. You'll also need something to cut out the hole in the middle—a narrow shot glass, for instance.

# Yeasted Waffles

2 teaspoons active dry yeast
½ cup warm water
1½ cups sorghum flour
½ cup brown rice flour
½ cup almond meal
½ cup tapioca starch
1 tablespoon white sugar
½ teaspoon salt
2 cups unsweetened soymilk
6 tablespoons butter (¾ stick), melted
2 large eggs

1. In a small bowl, mix the yeast with the warm water and let sit for 10 minutes to proof.
2. Meanwhile, thoroughly whisk together the flours, almond meal, starch, sugar, and salt in a large nonreactive bowl. Stir in the milk and butter. Add the yeast mixture and stir to combine. Cover and refrigerate overnight.
3. In the morning, remove the batter from the refrigerator, and let sit at room temperature for 30-45 minutes. Preheat a waffle iron.
4. Lightly beat the eggs in a small bowl, and then stir into the batter.
5. Once the waffle iron is hot, spoon in an appropriate amount of batter. Cook until desired doneness.
6. Repeat until all of the batter is used. Serve warm with your favorite toppings.

Makes approximately 8 7-inch waffles

I like to set the cooked waffles on a cooling rack instead of a plate to retain crispiness.

# Ful Medames
# (Egyptian Fava Beans)

2 15-ounce cans small fava beans (approximately 3½ cups), drained and rinsed
¾ cup gluten-free vegetable broth or water
1 teaspoon ground cumin
salt
4-5 cloves garlic, minced
3 tablespoons freshly squeezed lemon juice
½ cup chopped fresh parsley
2 tablespoons extra virgin olive oil + more for drizzling

1. Place fava beans in a small to medium pot. Add the vegetable broth or water, cumin, and a large pinch of salt. Cover, bring to a boil, and then reduce heat to low. Simmer about 10 minutes. Remove from heat.
2. Mash half to three-fourths of the beans. Add the garlic, lemon juice, parsley, and oil. Mix well.
3. Transfer to a serving bowl and drizzle with additional oil, if desired. Eat plain or serve with gluten-free bread or pita.

Serves 4

I have only been able to locate the small fava beans in cans. If they cannot be found, kidney beans can be used as a substitute.

Some other accompaniments or additions to consider include: hard boiled eggs, chopped fresh tomatoes, lemon wedges, extra fresh parsley, tahini, chili pepper flakes, raw onion, or pickled vegetables.

# Pumpkin Cranberry Bread

⅓ cup light olive oil + more for the pan
½ cup potato starch
½ cup sorghum flour
¼ cup buckwheat flour
¼ cup brown rice flour
2 teaspoons baking powder
1 teaspoon baking soda
1 teaspoon ground cinnamon
½ teaspoon ground allspice
½ teaspoon xanthan gum
¼ teaspoon salt
1 cup pumpkin puree
¾ cup dark brown sugar
2 teaspoons vanilla extract
1 cup fresh or frozen cranberries, halved

1. Preheat the oven to 350°F. Lightly grease a 9×5-inch loaf pan.
2. Thoroughly whisk the starch, flours, baking powder, baking soda, cinnamon, allspice, xanthan gum, and salt in a medium bowl.
3. Stir the pumpkin puree, ⅓ cup oil, sugar, and vanilla in a large bowl. Add the dry ingredients and stir to combine. Gently fold in the cranberries.
4. Pour the batter into the prepared loaf pan. Bake for about 60 minutes, until a toothpick inserted in the center comes out clean.

5. Set pan on a cooling rack. Once cool enough to handle, run a knife around the edge and turn the bread out onto the rack. Allow to cool completely before slicing.

Makes approximately 8 slices

If using frozen berries, there is no need to thaw first.

# Blueberry Coconut Granola

1½ cups gluten-free rolled oats
1 cup unsweetened shredded coconut
1 cup slivered almonds
1 cup chopped pecans
¼ cup olive oil
¼ cup honey
2 tablespoons light brown sugar
½ cup gluten-free oat flour
1 teaspoon orange extract
1 cup coarsely chopped dates
1 cup dried blueberries

1. Preheat the oven to 300°F.
2. Combine the rolled oats, coconut, almonds, and pecans in a large bowl.
3. In a small pot, heat the oil, honey, and sugar over medium heat until simmering, about 2 minutes. Remove from heat, and whisk in the oat flour and orange extract. Let cool slightly.
4. Pour the warm syrup over the oat and nut mixture, and mix well until evenly coated. Place on a large baking sheet and spread evenly.
5. Bake for 20 minutes, stir, then bake for another 20 minutes. Sprinkle dates and blueberries over the top and lightly press into the granola. Return to the oven and bake 5 minutes.

6. Allow to cool completely before breaking into pieces.

Makes approximately 9 cups

I think it's easiest to mix the syrup into the oat mixture by hand (after making sure the syrup is cool enough to handle), using a kneading motion until the oat mixture is thoroughly coated.

# Bagels

2 teaspoons active dry yeast
1½ cups warm water
1⅓ cups tapioca starch
1⅓ cups white rice flour
⅔ cup sorghum flour
⅔ cup almond meal
2 tablespoons light brown sugar
2 tablespoons psyllium husks
1 teaspoon salt + more for salting the water

1. Mix the yeast and the warm water. Let sit for 10 minutes to proof.
2. Thoroughly combine the starch, flours, almond meal, sugar, psyllium husk, and salt in the bowl of a stand mixer. Add the yeast mixture to the dry ingredients and mix on low speed until a dough forms, scraping down the sides as needed.
3. Grease a large bowl. Form the dough into a ball, set in the oiled bowl and turn to coat the entire ball with oil. Cover with a tea towel and set in a warm place for 1 hour. Dough should rise slightly.
4. Preheat the oven to 425°F. Line a large baking sheet with parchment paper. Bring a large pot of liberally salted water to boil.
5. Split the dough into 8 even segments. Roll one segment into a ball then slightly flatten. Poke a hole in the middle and stretch the hole slightly to form a bagel shape.

Set on a floured surface. Repeat with remaining pieces of dough.

6. Drop bagels into the boiling water a few at a time. Boil 2 minutes, flip, and boil 2 minutes more. Remove with a slotted spoon, drain, and place on the prepared baking sheet.

7. When all the bagels have been boiled, bake for 30-35 minutes, until golden-brown. Serve warm.

Makes 8 bagels

# Cinnamon Quinoa Muffins

½ cup sorghum flour
¼ cup potato starch
¼ cup almond meal
2 teaspoons baking powder
1½ teaspoons ground cinnamon
1 teaspoon xanthan gum
pinch crushed cardamom (seeds from 2 pods)
salt
2 large eggs
½ cup white sugar
3 tablespoons unsweetened soymilk
2 tablespoons light olive oil
1 teaspoon vanilla extract
¾ cup cooked quinoa

1. Preheat the oven to 350°F. Line a 12-cup muffin tin with baking cups.
2. Thoroughly whisk the flour, starch, almond meal, baking powder, cinnamon, xanthan gum, cardamom, and a pinch of salt in a medium bowl.
3. In a large bowl, lightly beat the eggs. Stir in the sugar, milk, oil, and vanilla. Add the dry mixture and the cooked quinoa. Stir well. Spoon the batter evenly between the prepared cups.

4. Bake for 25 minutes. Once the muffins are cool enough to touch, remove them from the tin and place on a cooling rack.

Makes 12 muffins

# Orange Sour Cream Coffee Cake

*Streusel Topping*
½ cup brown sugar
½ cup pecans, chopped
2 tablespoons brown rice flour
1 teaspoon ground cinnamon
4 tablespoons butter (½ stick), room temperature, cut into pieces

*Coffee Cake*
4 tablespoons butter (½ stick), room temperature + more for the pan
½ cup sorghum flour
½ cup brown rice flour
½ cup potato starch
½ cup almond meal
1 teaspoon baking powder
1 teaspoon baking soda
½ teaspoon xanthan gum
½ teaspoon salt
¾ cup white sugar
2 large eggs, room temperature
1 cup sour cream
zest of 1 medium orange
½ teaspoon orange extract

1. For the streusel topping, whisk together the sugar, pecans, flour, and cinnamon in a small bowl. Add the butter pieces and mix by hand to make a coarse meal.
2. Preheat the oven to 350°F. Grease an 8×8-inch baking dish or 9-inch round pan.
3. For the coffee cake, whisk together the flours, starch, almond meal, baking powder, baking soda, xanthan gum, and salt in a medium bowl. Cream the 4 tablespoons butter and the sugar in the bowl of a stand mixer on medium speed until light and fluffy. Add in the eggs, one at a time, mixing after each addition.
4. Add one-third of the flour mixture, half the sour cream, and mix. Add one-third of the flour mixture, the remaining half of the sour cream, and mix. Add the final one-third of the flour mixture, the zest, and the extract. Mix to fully incorporate.
5. Spoon half of the batter into the prepared baking dish. Top with half of the streusel. Spoon in the rest of the batter, then top with the remaining streusel. Bake about 45 minutes, until a toothpick inserted in the center comes out clean. Allow to cool before slicing.

Serves 8

Orange extract is best to boost the orange flavor, but vanilla extract can be substituted.

# Thick and Fluffy
# Buttermilk Pancakes

½ cup + 1 tablespoon tapioca starch
½ cup sorghum flour
⅓ cup brown rice flour
⅓ cup almond meal
2 tablespoons white sugar
2 teaspoons baking powder
1 teaspoon salt
¼ teaspoon xanthan gum
2 large eggs, room temperature
1 cup buttermilk
4 tablespoons butter (½ stick), melted
1 teaspoon vanilla extract
olive oil for the griddle

1. In a small bowl, whisk together the starch, flours, almond meal, sugar, baking powder, salt, and xanthan gum.
2. Whisk the eggs in a large bowl. Stir in the buttermilk, butter, and vanilla. Add the flour mixture and stir until just incorporated.
3. Preheat a griddle over medium heat. Use a towel to wipe a thin layer of oil onto the griddle. Lower heat just slightly. Drop batter by the large spoonful onto the griddle, using the spoon to spread the batter a bit. Cook about 3-4 minutes, until golden-brown. Flip and cook

another 3-4 minutes, until set. Repeat with remaining batter, reheating the griddle back to medium between batches. Serve with pure maple syrup.

Makes 12-14 4-inch pancakes

# Baked Eggs over Mushrooms and Onions

olive oil for the pan
1 medium yellow onion, cut in half, then sliced root to stem
1 pound crimini mushrooms, sliced
¼ teaspoon dried rosemary
pinch crushed red pepper
salt
4 large eggs

1. Preheat the oven to 350°F.
2. Heat a medium oven-safe pan over medium heat. Lightly coat the pan with oil. Add the onion and cook, stirring frequently, until golden and browning on the edges, 7-8 minutes.
3. Add the mushrooms, rosemary, red pepper, and a couple of large pinches of salt. Let mushrooms release their juices, then cook, stirring occasionally, until the liquid has boiled off, 10-15 minutes. Scrape the bottom of the pan to pick up any brown bits. Remove from heat.
4. Make four slight depressions in the mushrooms. Crack the eggs into the four depressions, taking care to not break the yolk.

5. Place the pan in the oven and bake until the egg whites are set; 8 minutes for runny yolks, 10 minutes for mostly set, 12 minutes for set.

Serves 4

# Gooey Butter Cake

*Crust*
4 tablespoons butter (½ stick), room temperature + more for the pan
3 tablespoons warm unsweetened soymilk
1 teaspoon active dry yeast
6 tablespoons tapioca starch
¼ cup sorghum flour
¼ cup brown rice flour
½ teaspoon xanthan gum
2 tablespoons white sugar
½ teaspoon salt
1 large egg

*Filling*
⅓ cup tapioca starch
⅓ cup sorghum flour
2 tablespoons brown rice flour
1 teaspoon xanthan gum
8 tablespoons butter (1 stick), room temperature
1 cup white sugar
¼ teaspoon salt
1 large egg
3 tablespoons light corn syrup
2 teaspoons vanilla extract
powdered sugar, for garnish

1. For the crust, mix the milk and yeast in a small bowl. Let sit for 10 minutes to proof. Grease an 8×8-inch baking dish that is at least 2 inches deep.
2. In another small bowl, thoroughly whisk together the starch, flours, and xanthan gum.
3. In a stand mixer, cream the butter, sugar, and salt. Scrape down the sides of the bowl and beat in the egg. Add the flour and milk mixtures and mix until thoroughly incorporated.
4. Spread the dough into the prepared baking dish. Cover the dish with plastic wrap or a lightweight towel, put in a warm place, and let rise for 1 hour.
5. Preheat the oven to 325°F.
6. For the filling, thoroughly whisk together the starch, flours, and xanthan gum in a small bowl.
7. In a stand mixer, cream the butter, sugar, and salt until light and fluffy, about 5 minutes. Scrape down the sides of the bowl and thoroughly beat in the egg for 3-4 minutes. Add the flour mixture, corn syrup, and vanilla. Beat until incorporated.
8. Gently spread the filling in an even layer over the crust. Bake for 40-45 minutes. Cake should be golden-brown around the edges, and just beginning to show brown spots in the middle. Allow to cool completely in pan.
9. Sprinkle with powdered sugar before serving.

Serves 8-10

This is a local specialty from my hometown (St. Louis). While it says cake in the title, most people eat gooey butter cake for breakfast, usually as a special treat on the weekends.

# Potatoes O'Brien

olive oil for the pan
½ medium yellow onion, diced
½ medium green bell pepper, cut into ½-inch pieces
½ medium red bell pepper, cut into ½-inch pieces
1 medium Yukon Gold potato (½ pound), cut into ½-inch cubes
salt and freshly ground black pepper

1. Heat a large pan with a lid over medium heat. Lightly coat the pan with oil. Add the onion and cook for 2-3 minutes, until translucent. Add the peppers and fry another 4-5 minutes, until softened. Set aside in a bowl.
2. Reduce heat to medium-low. Coat the pan with a thin layer of oil. Add the potatoes, stir well, then spread in an even layer, and cover. Cook for 5 minutes, stir, cover, and cook another 5 minutes. Stir, cover, and cook a final 5 minutes.
3. Remove lid, increase the heat to medium. Cook another 5-6 minutes, stirring once or twice, until the potatoes are lightly browned.
4. Return the cooked peppers and onion to the pan. Season with salt and pepper to taste. Allow to heat through, 1-2 minutes. Serve warm.

Serves 4-6

# Snacks and Appetizers

# Brussels Sprout Stuffed Onions

4 small-medium yellow onions (⅓ pound each)
olive oil
¼ pound Brussels sprouts, ends trimmed, diced
2 cloves garlic, finely minced
¼ cup fresh gluten-free bread crumbs
3 tablespoons mayonnaise or Vegenaise
1 tablespoon finely chopped fresh dill
1 tablespoon prepared horseradish
salt and freshly ground black pepper

1. Preheat the oven to 375°F.
2. Trim the ends off of the onions and cut in half horizontally (not root to stem). Remove the skin from the onions and pull or cut out the inner layers of the onions, leaving 3-4 layers (about ½-inch of onion). Rub each onion all over with oil. Set on a baking sheet and cover the sheet with aluminum foil. Bake for 30 minutes.
3. In a medium bowl, stir together the Brussels sprouts, garlic, bread crumbs, mayonnaise or Vegenaise, dill, and horseradish. Season to taste with salt and pepper.
4. Spoon the Brussels sprout mixture into the middle of each onion. Return to the oven and bake, uncovered, for 30 minutes.

Serves 4-8

# Veggie Snack Mix

10 radishes (½ pound without tops)
2 small Pink Lady apples (⅔ pound)
2 small turnips (½ pound), peeled
4 teaspoons paprika
2 teaspoons garlic powder
2 teaspoons freshly cracked black pepper
1 teaspoon onion powder
½ teaspoon dry mustard powder
½ teaspoon dried thyme
½ teaspoon dried oregano
½ teaspoon celery salt
½ teaspoon salt
¼ teaspoon ground cayenne pepper
½ cup cashews
2 teaspoons olive oil

1. Preheat the oven to 250°F.
2. Trim the ends off the radishes and thinly slice root to tip. Core the apples and thinly slice into pieces the same size as the radish slices. Trim the ends off the turnips and thinly slice into pieces the same size as the radish slices.
3. Mix all spices, herbs, salts, and pepper in a small bowl.
4. Place the radishes, apples, turnips and cashews in a large bowl. Drizzle with the oil and toss to coat. Add the spice mixture and toss to coat. Spread on two large baking sheets in a single layer.

5. Bake for 1 hour. Remove from the oven, stir, and spread the mixture into a single layer. Return to the oven, switching the racks the baking sheets were on, and bake 1 hour. Switch the baking sheets between racks once more, and bake 15-20 minutes. If the veggies and fruit start to look brown at any point, remove from the oven. The chips will harden as they cool.

Makes 7 cups

Keeping the radish, turnip, and apple pieces the same size is important to ensure they are equally crispy. I used Pink Lady apples because they are firm and not too juicy. If you cannot find them, substitute any other not-so-juicy apple.

This snack mix is fairly spicy. You can leave out the cayenne to avoid some of the heat.

# Tea Eggs

6 large eggs
½ cup gluten-free soy sauce or tamari
4 bags of black tea
3 star anise
1 stick cinnamon
1 tablespoon white sugar

1. Place the eggs in a medium pot. Fill with cold water to cover the eggs by about 1 inch.
2. Bring the water to a boil. Reduce the heat to low and simmer for 2½ minutes. Remove the eggs from the water and place in an ice bath or run under cold water.
3. Once eggs are cool enough to be handled, crack the shells all over using the back of a knife or the side of a spoon.
4. Place the eggs back in the hot water and add the remaining ingredients.
5. Bring the pot back to a boil, then reduce the heat to low and simmer 1-3 hours. Turn off heat. When the pot has cooled, cover and refrigerate overnight.
6. Peel and eat. The unpeeled eggs will keep for about 4 days in the liquid.

Makes 6 eggs

The longer the eggs are simmered the more flavorful they will be. The difference is more noticeable right after simmering, but even holds up after soaking overnight. However, the yolks of the longer simmered eggs are bluer around the edges, and have more of a sulfur taste, which dissipates slightly after the overnight soak.

# Broccoli Cheddar Muffins

¼ cup olive oil + more for the muffin tin and pan
½ medium yellow onion, diced
1 cup sorghum flour
½ cup almond meal
½ cup potato starch
1 teaspoon baking powder
½ teaspoon salt
1 large egg
1 cup unsweetened soymilk
¼ cup small broccoli florets
3 ounces shredded cheddar cheese (1 cup)
freshly ground black pepper

1. Preheat the oven to 350°F. Grease a 12-cup muffin tin.
2. Heat a medium pan over medium heat. Lightly coat the pan with oil. Once the oil is hot, add the onion. Sauté for a few minutes, until the onion is softened.
3. Stir together the flour, almond meal, starch, baking powder, and salt in a medium bowl.
4. In a large bowl, whisk together the egg, milk, and ¼ cup oil. Add the flour mixture and stir until just combined. Gently fold in the broccoli, cooked onion, cheese, and a few grinds of pepper. Spoon the batter into the prepared muffin cups.
5. Bake for about 30 minutes, until a toothpick inserted in a muffin comes out clean. Once the muffins are cool

enough to handle, remove from the tin and set on a cooling rack to cool completely.

Makes 12 muffins

# Apricot Pistachio Energy Bars

6 ounces dried apricots
¾ cup shelled pistachios
salt (optional)
10 ounces pitted dates

1. Place the apricots and pistachios (and a couple of pinches of salt if using) in a food processor and pulse until finely ground. Place in a large bowl.
2. Place the dates in the food processor and pulse until they form a large ball. Add the dates to the bowl and knead, like dough, until the apricots and pistachios are thoroughly incorporated. Form into a cylinder.
3. Lay out a piece of plastic wrap about 1½ feet long. Place the cylinder on the plastic wrap and fold the plastic wrap over in thirds. Use a rolling pin to roll into a large rectangle a little longer than a foot and about ½-inch thick. Cut horizontally into 12 bars.

Makes 12 bars

This recipe is very easy to customize with the fruit and nuts of your choice. The dates are important though to hold everything together. I usually use salted pistachios, avoiding the need for extra salt, but I would encourage a couple of pinches if your pistachios are unsalted.

# Baked Polenta Fries

olive oil for the baking sheet
2 cups gluten-free vegetable broth
¾ cup finely ground polenta (cornmeal)
½ teaspoon ground cumin
¼ teaspoon garlic powder
¼ teaspoon paprika
¼ teaspoon dried oregano
2 tablespoons nutritional yeast

1. Preheat the oven to 400°F. Grease a large baking sheet. Place the broth in a medium pot and set over high heat.
2. In a small bowl, stir together the polenta, spices, and nutritional yeast.
3. Once the broth is simmering, reduce the heat to medium. While stirring, slowly pour the polenta mixture into the pot. Cook, stirring continuously, until the broth is absorbed and the polenta is stiff. With finely ground polenta this should only take a few minutes; coarsely ground polenta will take longer.
4. Turn the polenta out onto the baking sheet and spread into ¼-inch thickness. Allow to cool about 10 minutes. Cut into strips about ¾-inch wide and a few inches long. Space the strips out so they are not touching. Bake for 20 minutes. Flip the fries over, and bake for another 20 minutes. Serve warm.

Serves 4

# Rosemary Raisin Millet Mini-Toasts

olive oil for the pan and baking sheet
1¼ cups sorghum flour
1 cup tapioca starch
½ cup almond meal
2 teaspoons dried rosemary, crushed
1½ teaspoons xanthan gum
1 teaspoon salt
¾ teaspoons baking soda
1¾ cups buttermilk
½ cup blackstrap molasses
1 cup raisins, chopped
¼ cup millet

1. Preheat the oven to 375°F. Grease a 9×5-inch loaf pan.
2. Whisk the flour, starch, almond meal, rosemary, xanthan gum, salt, and baking soda together in a large bowl. Make a well in the middle of the dry ingredients. Whisk the buttermilk and molasses together in the well, then stir into the dry ingredients. Stir in the raisins and millet.
3. Pour the batter into the prepared loaf pan. Smooth down, then lightly score lengthwise along the top of the batter.
4. Bake for 60 minutes, until a toothpick inserted into the center comes out clean. Allow to cool slightly, then run

a knife around the edge of the pan and turn the bread out onto a wire rack to cool completely.

5. Once the bread is cool, preheat the oven to 400°F. Grease a large baking sheet.
6. Slice the bread ¼-inch thick, then cut each piece in half. Lay each piece flat on the baking sheet. Bake for 10-12 minutes per side. Repeat until all of the loaf has been toasted.

Makes approximately 40 mini-toasts

When baking the mini-toasts, 10 minutes per side will produce a chewy center, while 12 minutes per side will provide crunch all the way through. These pair nicely with a mild cheese like Brie or Havarti.

# Sauerkraut Apple Fritters

peanut or vegetable oil for frying
¼ cup brown rice flour
¼ cup potato starch
¼ cup almond meal
2 teaspoons mustard seeds
½ teaspoon baking powder
pinch crushed cardamom seeds (seeds from 2 pods)
¼ cup unsweetened soymilk
1 large egg
1¼ cups sauerkraut, drained
1 medium Granny Smith apple (½ pound), diced
¼ cup dried cherries, diced

1. Lay out paper towels near to the stove. Add about 2 inches of oil to a wok or heavy-bottomed pot. Heat the oil to 350°F.
2. Whisk together the flour, starch, almond meal, mustard seeds, baking powder, and cardamom in a large bowl.
3. Whisk the milk and egg together in a small bowl. Right before the oil reaches the proper temperature, stir the egg mixture into the dry mix. Stir in the sauerkraut, apple, and cherries.
4. Drop tablespoons of the batter into the hot oil, 3 or 4 at a time, taking care not to overcrowd the pot. Fry for about 1½ minutes per side, until golden. Remove and set on the paper towels to absorb excess oil. Make sure

the oil comes back to 350°F before adding the next set of fritters.

Makes approximately 25 fritters

It may not look like the batter will hold together, but the egg and flour puff up as they cook. To avoid loose pieces, pack the batter into the tablespoon before dropping it in the oil.

If you're leery of sauerkraut, don't let that stop you from trying this recipe. The sauerkraut is not very potent.

# White Bean Millet Mini-Casseroles

olive oil for the pan and muffin tin
1 large yellow onion, diced
1½ cups + 2 tablespoons gluten-free hard pear cider or vegetable broth, divided
½ cup millet
2 bay leaves
salt
2 15-ounce cans cannellini beans (approximately 3½ cups), drained and rinsed
1 cup chopped curly endive/frisée
1 heaping tablespoon fresh thyme
1 tablespoon extra virgin olive oil
freshly ground black pepper

1. Heat a large pan over medium heat. Lightly coat the pan with oil. Add the onion and cook for about 5 minutes. Reduce the heat to medium-low and cook, stirring occasionally, until the onion is golden-brown, 45-50 minutes.
2. Meanwhile, place the 1½ cups cider or vegetable broth, millet, and bay leaves in a small pot. Add a pinch of salt. Cover and bring to a boil, then reduce the heat to low and simmer for 20-30 minutes, until the liquid is absorbed.
3. Preheat the oven to 350°F. Grease a 12-cup muffin tin.
4. Combine the beans, caramelized onion, endive, thyme, remaining 2 tablespoons of cider or vegetable broth, and

1 tablespoon of olive oil in a food processor. Process until smooth.

5. In a large mixing bowl, combine the bean puree with the cooked millet. Season to taste with salt and pepper. Spoon into the prepared muffin cups. Cover the tin with aluminum foil.

6. Bake for 20 minutes. Remove the foil and bake for another 10 minutes, until the edges are just beginning to brown. Remove from the oven, and let cool completely before removing from the tin.

Makes 12 mini-casseroles

# Squash-Wrapped Green Beans

2 tablespoons orange juice
2 tablespoons olive oil
1 tablespoon dark rum
2 teaspoons brown sugar
2 teaspoons gluten-free soy sauce or tamari
¼ teaspoon liquid smoke
¼ teaspoon crushed red pepper
1 medium yellow summer squash (½ pound), ends trimmed
¼ pound green beans, ends trimmed

1. Combine the orange juice, olive oil, rum, sugar, soy sauce or tamari, liquid smoke, and crushed red pepper in a flat wide vessel, like an 8×8-inch casserole dish. Whisk until the sugar is dissolved.
2. Lightly peel the skin from the squash. Peel strips of squash lengthwise and place in the marinade. Let sit for 30 minutes.
3. Preheat the oven to 375°F.
4. Wrap strips of marinated squash around individual green beans, leaving ½-inch at each end. Place on a large baking sheet. Continue until all green beans and squash have been used. Bake for 25-30 minutes. Serve warm.

Serves 4-6

# Buffalo Okra Bites

olive oil for the baking sheet
⅔ cup unsweetened soymilk
⅔ cup gluten-free buffalo hot sauce
½ pound okra, stems removed, cut into 1-inch sections
1½ cups finely ground Rice Chex crumbs

1. Preheat the oven to 350°F. Grease a large baking sheet.
2. Mix the milk and buffalo sauce in a medium bowl. Add the okra and toss to coat. Let sit 15 minutes.
3. Set the Chex crumbs in a wide, shallow bowl. Remove sections of okra and shake off any excess sauce. Roll in the crumbs until completely coated, then set on the baking sheet. Repeat until all okra has been used. Bake for 30 minutes. Serve warm.

Makes approximately 3 cups

# Soups and a Bread

# Dill Pickle Soup

olive oil for the pan
½ medium yellow onion, diced
2-3 cloves garlic, minced
3 medium Yukon Gold potatoes (1½ pounds), cubed
2½ cups gluten-free vegetable broth or water
½ cup pickle brine
8 ounces dill pickle spears (7-8 spears), diced + extra for garnish (optional)
¼ cup chopped fresh dill + extra for garnish (optional)

1. Heat a medium pot with a lid over medium heat. Lightly coat the bottom of the pot with oil. Add the onion and cook for 4-5 minutes, until softened. Add the garlic and cook until fragrant, around 30-60 seconds.
2. Add the potatoes, broth or water, and pickle brine. Cover and bring to a boil. Reduce the heat to a simmer and cook until the potatoes are tender, 15-20 minutes.
3. Pour the soup into a blender, or use an immersion blender to puree. If using a standing blender, remove the middle piece from the lid and cover with a towel to allow steam to escape while blending.
4. Return the soup to the pot. Stir in the pickles and dill. Cook until heated through, about 5 minutes. Serve immediately, garnished with extra pickles or dill, if desired.

Serves 4

# Butternut Squash Apple Soup

olive oil for the pot
1 medium yellow onion, diced
2 tablespoons minced ginger
2-pound butternut squash, peeled and cubed
4 medium Gala apples (2 pounds), cored and cubed
3 cups water
¼ teaspoon crushed red pepper
salt
pepitas (optional)

1. Heat a medium to large pot over medium heat. Lightly coat the bottom of the pot with oil. Add the onion and ginger and cook for 5 minutes, until softened.
2. Add the squash, then the apples and water. Season with crushed red pepper and a couple of pinches of salt. (The squash needs to be completely submerged. The apples do not.) Cover and bring to a boil. Reduce the heat to a simmer and cook for about 25 minutes, until the squash is easily pricked with a knife.
3. Pour the soup into a blender, or use an immersion blender to puree. If using a standing blender, remove the middle piece from the lid and cover with a towel to allow steam to escape while blending. Serve immediately, garnished with pepitas if desired.

Serves 6-8

Any sweet apple should work here. I like to increase the spiciness by adding a few squirts of sriracha on top.

# Borscht (Beet Soup)

5-6 medium beets (1½ pounds), ends trimmed
olive oil for the pot
1 medium yellow onion, diced
6 cups gluten-free vegetable broth or water
salt (if using water)
¼ cup freshly squeezed lemon juice
2-3 tablespoons chopped fresh dill

1. Peel the beets, then shred using a box grater or food processor.
2. Heat a medium to large pot over medium heat. Lightly coat the bottom of the pot with oil. Add the onion and cook, stirring occasionally, until tender, golden, and just beginning to brown, 7-8 minutes.
3. Add the beets and the broth or water to the pot. (If using water, add a few large pinches of salt.) Increase the heat to high, cover, and bring to a boil. Reduce the heat to low and simmer, covered, until the beets are completely tender, 45-60 minutes.
4. Remove the soup from the heat and stir in the lemon juice and dill. Allow the pot to cool to room temperature then place in the refrigerator to cool completely. Serve chilled.

Serves 4-6

Some other accompaniments or additions to consider include: kefir, sour cream or plain yogurt, hard boiled eggs, chilled boiled potatoes, or lemon wedges.

# Grapefruit Edamame Soup

olive oil for the pot
1 medium yellow onion, diced
1½ pounds shelled edamame
1 medium Yukon Gold potato (½ pound), peeled and cubed
3 cups gluten-free vegetable broth
1 cup freshly brewed green tea
freshly ground black pepper
½ cup freshly squeezed grapefruit juice
zest of 1 medium grapefruit, divided

1. Heat a medium pot over medium heat. Lightly coat the bottom of the pot with oil, and add the onion. Cook for a few minutes, until softened.
2. Add the edamame, potatoes, broth, and tea. Add a generous amount of pepper. Cover, bring to a boil, then reduce the heat to low and let simmer for 20 minutes, until the potatoes and edamame are tender.
3. Add the grapefruit juice and half of the grapefruit zest. Pour the soup into a blender, or use an immersion blender to puree. If using a standing blender, remove the middle piece from the lid and cover with a towel to allow steam to escape while blending. Allow the pot to cool to room temperature, then refrigerate until completely cooled.
4. Serve chilled and garnish with the remaining grapefruit zest.

Serves 6

Shelled edamame can usually be found in the frozen vegetable section of the grocery store.

When brewing the tea, be sure not to brew for too long as doing so results in bitter tea, which will make the soup bitter as well.

# Cauliflower Corn Chowder

3 tablespoons butter
½ medium yellow onion, diced
2 tablespoons sorghum flour
1 tablespoon tapioca starch
3 cups medium cauliflower florets
1 medium Yukon Gold potato (½ pound), cut into ½-inch cubes
3 cups gluten-free vegetable broth
¼ teaspoon crushed red pepper
1½ cups fresh or frozen corn (2-3 ears)
1 cup whipping cream
salt and freshly ground black pepper

1. Melt the butter in a medium pot over medium heat. Add the onion and cook for 3 minutes, until softened.
2. Add the flour and starch and cook another 3 minutes, stirring frequently, until light brown.
3. Add the cauliflower, potato, broth, and red pepper. Cover and bring to a boil, then reduce the heat to a simmer and cook, covered, for 15 minutes.
4. Add the corn, then cover and cook for 5 minutes. Add the cream, then cover and cook another 5 minutes, until heated through. Add salt and pepper to taste. Serve hot.

Serves 4-6

If using frozen corn, thaw before adding to the soup.

# Vegetable "Barley" Soup

olive oil for the pot
½ medium yellow onion, diced
3-4 cloves garlic, minced
2 medium carrots (¼ pound), ends trimmed, cut into ½-inch pieces
2 medium stalks celery, ends trimmed, cut into ½-inch pieces
⅓ pound green beans, ends trimmed, cut into 1-inch pieces
1 small turnip (¼ pound), ends trimmed, cut into ½-inch cubes
3 cups gluten-free vegetable broth
1 28-ounce can crushed tomatoes
¼ teaspoon crushed red pepper
½ cup gluten-free steel-cut oats

1. Heat a medium to large pot over medium heat. Lightly coat the bottom of the pot with oil. Add the onion and garlic. Cook about 3 minutes, until the onion softens.
2. Add the carrots, celery, green beans, turnip, broth, tomatoes, and red pepper. Cover and bring to a boil, then reduce the heat to low and simmer for 40-45 minutes.
3. Add the oats and cook, covered, for 20-30 minutes, until the oats are soft. Serve immediately.

Serves 6-8

Note that the oats continue to absorb liquid. If you're going to let the soup simmer longer or you plan to store some soup for later, you will need to add more liquid.

# White Chili

2 cups dried great northern beans, picked through
olive oil for the pot
1 medium yellow onion, diced
1 poblano pepper, seeds removed, minced
1 Anaheim pepper, seeds removed, minced
1 serrano pepper, seeds removed, minced
5-6 cloves garlic, minced
1½ teaspoons dried oregano
1 teaspoon ground cumin
4 cups gluten-free vegetable broth or water
salt (if using water)

1. Place the great northern beans in a large bowl or pot and cover with cool water. Soak overnight. When ready to start the chili, drain and rinse.
2. Heat a medium to large pot over medium heat. Lightly coat the bottom of the pot with olive oil. Add the onion and cook a few minutes, until softened. Add the peppers and garlic and cook for another 3-4 minutes, until softened.
3. Add the soaked beans, oregano, cumin and broth or water. (If using water add a few large pinches of salt.) Cover and bring to a boil, then reduce the heat to low. Cook until the beans are tender, 1½-2 hours.

Serves 4-6

This recipe can be made with unsoaked beans. Use 6 cups of water or broth and allow for 1 additional hour of cooking time.

Cannellini or navy beans can be substituted for the northern beans.

# Focaccia

2 teaspoons white sugar
1¼ cups warm water
1 tablespoon active dry yeast
1 cup tapioca starch
1 cup sorghum flour
¾ cup brown rice flour
½ cup almond meal
1 teaspoon xanthan gum
½ teaspoon salt
4 tablespoons light olive oil, divided + more for the pan
coarse salt (optional)

1. In a small bowl, stir the sugar into the warm water until dissolved. Add the yeast and let sit for 10 minutes, until the yeast is bubbly.
2. In a large bowl, thoroughly whisk together the starch, flours, almond meal, xanthan gum, and salt.
3. Add the yeast mixture and 2 tablespoons of the oil into the flour. Stir well.
4. Grease a 9×13-inch casserole dish. Press the dough into the casserole dish. Cover with a damp towel and allow the dough to rise in a warm place for 1 hour.
5. Preheat the oven to 400°F.
6. Drizzle the remaining 2 tablespoons of oil over the dough and spread to cover the entire surface. Use your fingertips to make deep indentations all over the dough. If desired, sprinkle with coarse salt. Bake for 20 minutes,

until browned around the edges, and the middle feels firm if lightly touched. Allow to cool slightly before slicing.

Serves 8

# Sides

# Pea and New Potato Salad

1 cup frozen peas
1 pound small red-skinned new potatoes
salt
2 tablespoons Greek yogurt
2 teaspoons freshly squeezed lemon juice
2 teaspoons extra virgin olive oil
2 teaspoons water
¼ medium red onion, diced
¼ cup fresh basil, thinly sliced
¼ cup fresh mint, thinly sliced
freshly ground black pepper

1. Set peas in a colander. Run under warm water. Let sit to defrost.
2. Scrub the potatoes and place in a medium pot. Cover with cold water and liberally salt. Bring to a boil, then reduce heat to low and simmer for 15-20 minutes, until the potatoes can be easily pierced with a fork. Drain.
3. Whisk the yogurt, lemon juice, oil, and water in a small bowl.
4. Once the potatoes are cool enough to handle, cut in quarters and place in a large bowl. Stir in the peas, onion, basil, mint, and dressing. Season with salt and pepper to taste.

Serves 4

# Braised Brussels Sprouts
# with Mustard Sauce

olive oil for the pan
1 large shallot, minced
1 pound Brussels sprouts, ends trimmed, sliced lengthwise into
4-5 slices
5 tablespoons water, divided
salt
¼ cup Dijon mustard
1 tablespoon brown sugar
freshly ground black pepper

1. Heat a large pan with a lid over medium heat. Lightly coat the pan with oil. Add the shallot and cook until softened, 2-3 minutes. Stir in the Brussels sprouts, 3 tablespoons of water, and a pinch of salt. Arrange the sprouts in an even layer. Reduce the heat to medium-low, cover, and cook for 5 minutes.
2. Meanwhile, whisk the mustard, sugar, and remaining 2 tablespoons of water together in a small bowl.
3. When ready, the sprouts should be bright green. Stir in the mustard sauce and a few cranks of black pepper. Cover, reduce the heat to low, and cook for 2-3 minutes.

Serves 4-6

This recipe results in Brussels sprouts with a bit of firmness in the middle. Cook a few minutes longer for completely tender sprouts.

# Sweet and Sour
# Bok Choy and Turnips

⅓ cup + 1 tablespoon water
⅓ cup rice vinegar
⅓ cup pineapple juice
2 tablespoons brown sugar
2 teaspoons gluten-free soy sauce or tamari
1 teaspoon finely minced ginger
pinch crushed red pepper
olive oil for the pan
2 small turnips (½ pound), ends trimmed, cut into ¼-inch matchsticks
½ medium white onion, thinly sliced root to stem
1 pound bok choy, thinly sliced
1 tablespoon cornstarch

1. Put the ⅓ cup water, vinegar, pineapple juice, sugar, soy sauce or tamari, ginger, and red pepper in a small pot. Set over medium-low heat.
2. Heat a large pan over high heat. Lightly coat the pan with oil. Add the turnips and onion and sauté for 4-5 minutes, until softened. Set aside in a bowl.
3. Lightly coat the pan with additional oil. Add the bok choy and cook for 4-5 minutes, until softened. Add the turnips and onions back to the pan, stir to combine, and remove from the heat.

4. By now the pineapple sauce should be simmering. Increase the heat to medium-high. Whisk the cornstarch with the remaining 1 tablespoon of water in a small bowl. Add the cornstarch slurry to the sauce and whisk briskly until the sauce thickens, about 30 seconds.
5. Add the sauce to the vegetables and stir to coat.

Serves 4

# Patatas Bravas
# (Potatoes with
# Spicy Dipping Sauce)

3 medium Yukon Gold potatoes (1½ pounds)
olive oil to drizzle and pan fry
4-5 cloves garlic, finely minced
1 8-ounce can tomato sauce
1½ teaspoons sherry vinegar
½ teaspoon paprika
heaping ¼ teaspoon crushed red pepper

1. Preheat the oven to 400°F. Cut the potatoes in fourths lengthwise, and then slice into 1-2 inch segments.
2. Arrange the potatoes on a baking sheet. Lightly drizzle with oil, and toss to coat. Bake for 45 minutes, stirring at 15-minute intervals.
3. Heat a small pot over medium heat. Lightly coat the bottom of the pot with oil. Add the garlic and sauté about 1 minute. Stir in the tomato sauce, vinegar, paprika, and red pepper. Reduce the heat to low and simmer until the potatoes are ready.
4. Serve the potato wedges with the sauce on the side for dipping.

Serves 4

Alternatively, you can mix the sauce with the potatoes; however, in doing so, you lose the crispiness of the potatoes.

# Braised Green Beans
# with Miso Glaze

olive oil for the pan
1 medium yellow onion, cut in half, then thinly sliced
root to stem
1 pound green beans, ends trimmed
freshly ground black pepper
½ cup water
1 tablespoon gluten-free light miso

1. Heat a large pan with a lid over medium-high heat. Lightly coat the pan with oil. Add the onion and cook for a few minutes, until starting to brown.
2. Stir in the green beans and a generous amount of pepper. Add the water, cover, and reduce the heat to medium-low. Cook, stirring once or twice, for about 30 minutes, until the green beans are tender.
3. Stir the miso into the pan juices, and then stir to coat the green beans.

Serves 4

# Maque Choux
# (Cajun Corn and Peppers)

olive oil for the pan
4¼ cups corn (6-7 ears)
2 medium stalks celery, ends trimmed, diced
½ medium red bell pepper, cut into ½-inch pieces
½ medium green bell pepper, cut into ½-inch pieces
½ medium yellow onion, diced
4-5 cloves garlic, minced
⅓ cup gluten-free vegetable broth
¼ teaspoon cayenne pepper
¼ teaspoon paprika
freshly ground black pepper
2 tablespoons chopped fresh parsley
1½ tablespoons chopped fresh oregano
¼ cup whipping cream

1. Heat a large pan with a lid over high heat. Generously coat the pan with oil. Add the corn, celery, bell peppers, onion, and garlic. Cook for 5 minutes then reduce the heat to medium-low. Stir in the vegetable broth, cayenne, paprika, and a generous amount of black pepper. Cover and let simmer for 30 minutes.
2. Stir in the parsley, oregano, and cream. Cover and let simmer for another 5 minutes.

Serves 4-6

# Broccoli Cauliflower
# Chopped Salad

*Salad*
olive oil for the pan
4 ounces tempeh, crumbled
salt
2 teaspoons liquid smoke
2½ cups diced broccoli
2½ cups diced cauliflower
3 small shallots, minced
¼ cup roasted sunflower seeds

*Dressing*
¾ cup mayonnaise or Vegenaise
¼ cup apple cider vinegar
¾ teaspoon garlic powder
¾ teaspoon dry mustard powder
salt and freshly ground black pepper

1. Heat a small pan over medium-high heat. Lightly coat the pan with oil. Add the tempeh and a few generous pinches of salt. Sauté for a few minutes, until browned. Add the liquid smoke in two additions, while stirring well. Cook 1 minute, then remove from the heat.
2. For the salad, add the broccoli, cauliflower, shallots, sunflower seeds, and the tempeh to a large bowl.
3. For the dressing, whisk together the mayonnaise or Vegenaise, vinegar, garlic, and mustard in a small bowl.

Pour over the salad and toss to coat. Season to taste with salt and pepper. Refrigerate for 1 hour before serving.

Serves 6-8

# Marinated Asparagus

1 pound asparagus, root ends trimmed
2 tablespoons orange juice
1 tablespoon extra virgin olive oil
1 tablespoon sherry
1 clove garlic, finely minced
salt and freshly ground black pepper

1. Salt a medium to large pot of water and bring to a boil. Add the asparagus and cook for 2 minutes, until bright green, but still lightly crisp. While the asparagus is cooking, prepare an ice bath. Drain the asparagus and immediately place in the ice bath to stop cooking. Once cooled, drain.

2. In a wide, shallow dish whisk together the orange juice, oil, sherry, and garlic. Season with salt and pepper to taste. Add the drained asparagus. Toss to coat and let marinate for 30 minutes, stirring once or twice.

Serves 4

The asparagus can be marinated longer, but I don't recommend refrigerating, as the garlic will overpower the other flavors if served cold.

# Braised Celery

1 head celery, ends trimmed
olive oil for the pan
½ medium yellow onion, diced
½ cup gluten-free vegetable broth
1 bay leaf
freshly ground black pepper
1 tablespoon Dijon mustard

1. Peel the strings from the celery stalks using a vegetable peeler or paring knife. Chop diagonally into 1-2 inch sections.
2. Heat a large pan with a lid over medium heat. Lightly coat the pan with oil. Add the onion and sauté for a few minutes, until translucent. Add the celery and sauté for 4-5 minutes. The celery will brighten in color.
3. Add the vegetable broth, bay leaf, and pepper to taste. Allow the broth to start to bubble, then reduce the heat to low and cover. Simmer the celery for 30 minutes. If desired softness is reached, continue to next step. If not, cover and simmer for another 10-15 minutes.
4. Uncover, discard the bay leaf and stir in the mustard. Return the heat to medium-high. Cook for 1-2 minutes to reduce the liquid to a thick glaze.

Serves 4

# Cornbread and Cornbread Stuffing

*Cornbread*
olive oil for the casserole dish
1 cup cornmeal
⅔ cup sorghum flour
⅓ cup potato starch
¼ cup white sugar
1½ teaspoons baking powder
1 teaspoon salt
¼ teaspoon xanthan gum
2 large eggs
1¼ cups buttermilk
2 tablespoons butter, melted

1. Preheat the oven to 375°F. Grease an 8×8-inch casserole dish.
2. Whisk together the cornmeal, flour, starch, sugar, baking powder, salt, and xanthan gum in a large bowl.
3. In a large mixing bowl, lightly beat the eggs. Stir in the buttermilk and butter. Add the dry ingredients and mix until just combined.
4. Pour the batter into the prepared baking dish. Bake for 35-40 minutes, until the cornbread is springy to the touch and a toothpick inserted in the middle comes out clean. Let cool completely before cutting.

Serves 4-6

*Cornbread Stuffing*
olive oil or butter for the casserole dish and pan
1 medium yellow onion, diced
2 small stalks celery, ends trimmed, diced
3-4 cloves garlic, minced
1 batch cornbread (from above)
1 tablespoon finely chopped fresh sage leaves
1½ teaspoons chopped fresh rosemary
¼ teaspoon crushed red pepper
1½ cups gluten-free vegetable broth
salt and freshly ground black pepper
1-2 tablespoons butter (optional)

1. Preheat the oven to 350°F. Grease a medium casserole dish (around 7×11-inch).
2. Heat a medium pan over medium heat. Lightly coat the pan with oil or butter. Add the onion and celery. Cook for 7-8 minutes, until softened, and then push the vegetables to one side of the pan. Add the garlic. Cook for 30-60 seconds. Stir into the onion and celery and remove the pan from the heat.
3. Crumble the cornbread into a large mixing bowl. Stir in the onion mixture, sage, rosemary, and red pepper. Add the vegetable broth and stir until all the cornbread is moistened. Season with salt and pepper to taste.
4. Spoon the stuffing into the prepared casserole dish. If desired, dot the top of the stuffing with 1-2 tablespoons

butter. Bake for 45 minutes, until the stuffing is just beginning to brown. Serve warm.

Serves 6

# Mains

# Corn Waffle Sandwiches

*For the Waffles*
½ cup tapioca starch
½ cup sorghum flour
¼ cup brown rice flour
¼ cup almond meal
1 teaspoon baking powder
½ teaspoon ground coriander
½ teaspoon salt
¾ cup unsweetened soymilk
¼ cup extra virgin olive oil
2 large eggs
1 cup corn (1-2 ears)
1 medium jalapeño pepper, seeds removed, minced

*Per Sandwich*
2-3 slices small tomato
¼ avocado, mashed
2 tablespoons sprouts
1 thinly sliced semicircle from half medium red onion

1. Preheat a waffle iron.
2. Whisk together the starch, flours, almond meal, baking powder, coriander, and salt in a large bowl. Stir in the milk and oil until just incorporated. Whisk the eggs in a small bowl until frothy, and then stir into the batter. Stir in the corn and jalapeño.
3. Spoon batter onto the waffle iron and cook until desired doneness. Repeat with remaining batter.

4. Take one quarter of a waffle, top with sliced tomato, avocado, sprouts, and sliced onion. Top with another quarter. Repeat with remaining waffles. Serve.

Makes 4 7-inch waffles - 8 sandwiches

Make sure to spoon the batter around the waffle iron, otherwise the corn and jalapeños clump in the middle.

# Pineapple Dal

2½ cups gluten-free vegetable broth
1 cup pineapple cut into ½-inch chunks (1 8-ounce can)
¾ cup split red lentils (masoor dal), picked through
2 teaspoons tamarind concentrate/paste
2 tablespoons coconut oil
¼ teaspoon cumin seeds
¼ teaspoon mustard seeds
½ medium yellow onion, minced
2 serrano peppers, seeds removed, minced
4 cloves garlic, minced
1 tablespoon minced ginger

1. Place the vegetable broth, pineapple, lentils, and tamarind concentrate in a medium pot. Cover and bring to a boil. Reduce the heat to low and simmer for 30 minutes, until the lentils are tender.
2. Once the lentils are cooked, heat the coconut oil in a medium pan over medium-high heat. Add the cumin and mustard seeds and cook until fragrant and beginning to pop, 30 seconds. Add the onion, peppers, garlic, and ginger and cook for 2 minutes, until the onion starts to brown. Stir into the lentils and serve.

Serves 4

The dal goes well with rice (especially basmati) or with gluten-free pita to scoop it up. If you'd like to increase the spiciness, leave the seeds in the peppers.

Tamarind is a fruit commonly used in Indian, Mexican, and a variety of Asian cuisines. I've had the best luck finding it in Asian grocery stores.

# Falafel

2 cups dried chickpeas, picked through
peanut oil or vegetable oil for frying
½ medium yellow onion, roughly chopped
5 cloves garlic, smashed
1 cup fresh parsley leaves
2 tablespoons tahini
1 tablespoon freshly squeezed lemon juice
2 teaspoons ground cumin
1 teaspoon ground coriander
1 teaspoon salt
½ teaspoon crushed red pepper
½ teaspoon baking soda
½ teaspoon freshly ground black pepper

1. Place the dried chickpeas in a large bowl or pot and cover with cool water. Soak for 18 to 24 hours. Drain and replace the water a couple of times during that period. The beans should double or triple in size.
2. Add about 2 inches of oil to a wok or heavy-bottomed pot. Heat the oil to 375°F. Set out layers of paper towels nearby.
3. Drain the beans and give them one final rinse. Put the beans and all remaining ingredients in a food processor. Pulse until the mixture is finely ground and some of the mixture is paste-like. Be sure to scrape down the sides and stir between pulses.

4. Drop by the tablespoon into the hot oil, 3-4 at a time, taking care not to overcrowd the pot. Fry 4-5 minutes per side, until dark brown. Remove and set on the paper towels to absorb excess oil. Make sure the oil comes back to 375°F before adding the next batch. Repeat until all the batter has been used.

Makes about 30 falafel

# Brussels Sprout Potato Frittata

olive oil for the pan
2 small Yukon Gold potatoes (½ pound), cut into ½-inch cubes
salt and freshly ground black pepper
½ medium yellow onion, diced
½ pound Brussels sprouts, ends trimmed, sliced in half lengthwise, then thinly sliced
8 large eggs
zest of 1 small lemon
1 tablespoon fresh tarragon, coarsely chopped

1. Heat a large oven-safe pan over medium-high heat. Generously coat the pan with oil. Add the potatoes. Sauté, stirring occasionally, until browned on the outside and just tender inside, about 10 minutes. Remove from the pan. Season with salt and pepper to taste.
2. Reduce the heat to medium. Add the onion and cook for 3 minutes, until softened. Add the Brussels sprouts and cook for 5-6 minutes, until bright green and just beginning to brown. Remove from the heat. Season with salt and pepper to taste.
3. Lightly beat the eggs in a large mixing bowl. Add the cooked potatoes, Brussels sprouts, onion, lemon zest, and tarragon and stir well.
4. Set the pan over medium-low heat. Lightly coat the pan with oil. Add the egg mixture, spreading the vegetables out to evenly distribute. Cook until almost all of the egg

is set, around 15 minutes. Place a rack in the middle of the oven, and turn the broiler on low. Place the frittata under the broiler until the remaining egg is set, about 5 minutes.

5. Run a spatula around the edges of the pan, gently lifting the frittata, until it is loose. Turn out onto a platter and cut into wedges.

Serves 8

# Black Bean Plantain Burgers

*Burgers*
1 medium plantain, peeled, cut into 1-inch pieces
salt
1 cup cooked black beans
½ medium red bell pepper, roughly chopped
½ medium green bell pepper, roughly chopped
4 cloves garlic, roughly chopped
2 small tomatillos, roughly chopped
2 small chipotles in adobo
¼ teaspoon ground cumin
¼ teaspoon dried oregano
½ cup crushed tortilla chips
olive oil for the pan or baking sheet

*Topping*
1½ avocados
½ mango, cut into small chunks (½ cup)
1 teaspoon freshly squeezed lime juice
salt

1. Put the plantain pieces in a medium pot. Cover with water and liberally salt. Cover and bring to a boil. Reduce the heat to a simmer and cook for 20-25 minutes, until the plantain can be easily pierced with a knife. Drain and let cool slightly.
2. Put the plantain in a food processor and quickly pulse a few times. Add the remaining burger ingredients, except the crushed tortilla chips. Pulse until a chunky paste

forms. Spoon into a large bowl and stir in the tortilla chips. Form into 8 patties.

3. For pan fried burgers, heat a large pan or griddle over medium-low heat. Lightly coat the pan with oil. Cook, about 20 minutes per side, until the patties are golden-brown and firm.

4. For baked burgers, lightly grease a baking sheet, and place the patties on the sheet. Place an oven rack in the middle of the oven. Set the broiler to low and broil the patties for 15-20 minutes per side, until browned and firm.

5. While the patties are cooking, prepare the topping. Cut the avocado in half and remove the pit. Score the inside flesh with a paring knife and remove the flesh with a spoon. Place in a bowl. Add the mango. Stir in the lime juice and season to taste with salt.

6. Serve the burgers with the avocado topping.

Makes 8 3-inch patties

These are between burgers and sliders in size. I wouldn't recommend making them bigger as they tend to fall apart at larger sizes.

It is easier to peel the plantain if it is lightly scored along its length first.

Look for canned chipotles in adobo in the Mexican food section of your grocery store.

# Roasted Portobello Mushrooms with Roasted Bell Peppers and Blue Cheese

4 portobello mushrooms, stems removed
¼ cup olive oil
¼ cup balsamic vinegar
4 cloves garlic, minced
1 teaspoon dried rosemary
salt and freshly ground black pepper
2 small red or orange bell peppers (¾ pound)
2 ounces gluten-free blue cheese, crumbled

1. Place mushrooms gill side up in a casserole dish. Cover evenly with the oil and vinegar. Divide the garlic and rosemary between the mushrooms and sprinkle generously with salt and pepper. Set aside to marinate for 1-2 hours.
2. Using tongs, roast the bell peppers over an open flame until the skin is blackened. Alternatively, cut peppers into quarters and place skin side up on a baking sheet. Place under a broiler until black all over. Once peppers are blackened, enclose them in a paper bag or covered dish to steam. When peppers are cool enough to handle, rub the outside with a towel to remove the blackened skin. Cut into thin strips.

3. Preheat the oven to 425°F. Roast the mushrooms for 20-25 minutes.
4. Remove the mushrooms from the oven and top each one with one-fourth of the peppers and ½ ounce of blue cheese. Return to the oven, and roast an additional 5 minutes, until the peppers are heated through. Serve immediately.

Serves 4

# Mujadara (Lentils and Rice with Frizzled Onion)

1 teaspoon olive oil + more for the pot
1 large yellow onion, one half diced, one half thinly sliced root to stem
3-4 cloves garlic, minced
1½ teaspoons ground cumin
½ teaspoon ground allspice
¼ teaspoon ground cinnamon
2 cups gluten-free vegetable broth
½ cup brown basmati rice
½ cup brown lentils, picked through
3 tablespoons fresh mint, thinly sliced

1. Heat a medium pot over medium-high heat. Lightly coat the bottom of the pot with oil. Add the diced onion and garlic. Cook for a few minutes, until the onion softens. Add the cumin, allspice, and cinnamon and cook until fragrant, about 15 seconds. Add the vegetable broth, rice, and lentils. Cover and bring to a boil. Reduce the heat to a simmer and let cook undisturbed for about 30-40 minutes.
2. While the lentils and rice are cooking, heat a medium pan over medium heat. Add the sliced onion. Cook, stirring frequently, for 5 minutes, until just starting to brown. Add the 1 teaspoon oil, and lower the heat

slightly to just under medium. Cook, stirring frequently, until the onion is brown and frizzled, about 15 minutes.

3. Check the lentils and rice. If the broth is absorbed, turn off the heat. If broth is not absorbed, cook another 5-10 minutes. Let sit, covered, for about 5 minutes.

4. Spoon the lentils and rice into bowls. Garnish with frizzled onion and fresh mint.

Serves 4

The amount of time it takes to cook the frizzled onion varies quite a bit. Keep an eye on it. Stirring frequently, especially once the onion starts to brown, helps to prevent burning.

# Chipotle Apricot Encrusted Cauliflower

2 tablespoons olive oil + more for the casserole dish
1 small head of cauliflower (2¼-2½ pounds)
1 small Bartlett pear, cut into large chunks
3 cloves garlic, roughly chopped
3-4 small chipotles in adobo sauce
6 ounces dried apricots
2 tablespoons honey

1. Preheat the oven to 425°F. Lightly grease an 8×8-inch casserole dish.
2. Remove the leaves and stalk of the cauliflower. Slightly cut into and remove a small portion of the core. Put the cauliflower core side up into the casserole dish.
3. Place the remaining ingredients in a food processor, and pulse until a thick paste forms. Spoon the apricot mixture into the crevices between the cauliflower florets. Lightly pat the filling around the bottom of the cauliflower. Flip the cauliflower over, and continue patting the apricot mixture onto the cauliflower, until it's completely coated. Loosely cover the dish with a piece of aluminum foil.
4. Bake for 1 hour. Remove the foil and bake for another 30 minutes, until a knife can easily be inserted in the center.

Serves 4-6

Look for canned chipotles in adobo in the Mexican food section of your grocery store.

# Sweet and Smoky
# Dry Rub Tofu

1 12-ounce block extra firm tofu
1 tablespoon brown sugar
2 teaspoons lapsang souchong tea, crushed to a powder
1½ teaspoons salt
1 teaspoon ground ginger
1 teaspoon garlic powder
½ teaspoon dry mustard powder
½ teaspoon ground cinnamon
½ teaspoon ground cloves
¼ teaspoon ground cumin
¼ teaspoon ground coriander
¼ teaspoon freshly ground black pepper
¼ teaspoon crushed red pepper
olive oil for the baking sheet

1. Rinse the tofu and pat dry. Slice the tofu widthwise into eight even slices.
2. Mix the sugar, tea, salt, and all of the spices in a small bowl. Rub the spice mixture onto the tofu slices, covering all sides.
3. Move your oven rack to its highest position. Turn the broiler on low.
4. Grease a baking sheet. Arrange the tofu slices on the sheet in a single layer and place under the broiler. Cook

for 11-12 minutes; the tofu should feel firm around the edges. Flip and cook for another 11-12 minutes.

Serves 2-4

Lapsang souchong is a smoke-dried Chinese tea, and the source of smokiness in this recipe. I use a coffee grinder to grind it into a powder.

It is important to pat the tofu dry. If it's too wet the rub doesn't stick as well.

# Spicy Sour Noodles

## Sauce
⅓ cup freshly squeezed lime juice
¼ cup gluten-free vegetable broth
4 teaspoons white sugar
2 serrano peppers, minced
1 teaspoon gluten-free soy sauce or tamari

## Noodles
½ pound Napa cabbage, cut in thirds lengthwise and thinly sliced
4 cups water
½ cup peanuts, finely chopped
4 ounces gluten-free bean thread noodles
¼ medium red onion, thinly sliced
¼ cup finely chopped fresh cilantro

1. Put the sauce ingredients in a bowl and stir until the sugar is dissolved.
2. Place the cabbage in a large bowl. Bring the water to a boil in a medium pot. Set a medium pan over medium heat. Add the peanuts to the pan. Cook, stirring frequently, until lightly browned, about 4-5 minutes.
3. Once the water is boiling, remove from the heat and add the noodles. Let sit for 5 minutes. Drain the noodles and use scissors to cut into smaller pieces. Add to the cabbage and immediately pour the sauce over the noo-

dles. Stir well. Add the onion, cilantro, and peanuts and stir until thoroughly combined.

Serves 6-8

This dish can be chilled and served cold. It is very spicy; to make it less spicy remove the seeds and membranes from inside the serrano peppers or use one fewer pepper. Using a vegetable broth that's lighter in color makes for a better-looking dish.

I prefer bean thread noodles to rice vermicelli as they clump less. Rice vermicelli can be used, but it is even more important to add the sauce quickly to keep the noodles from clumping. Look for either of them in the Asian section of your grocery store.

# Coconut Curry Stuffed Sweet Potatoes

3 medium sweet potatoes (1½ pounds)
olive oil for the potatoes and pan
3-4 teaspoons minced ginger
2-3 cloves garlic, minced
½ jalapeño pepper, minced
½ teaspoon dry mustard powder
¼ teaspoon ground turmeric
¼ teaspoon ground cumin
¼ teaspoon ground coriander
¼ teaspoon ground cinnamon
pinch crushed cardamom seeds (seeds from 2 pods)
2 cups de-stemmed chopped kale
½ cup full-fat canned coconut milk

1. Preheat the oven to 400°F. Scrub the outside of the sweet potatoes to remove any dirt. Pat dry. Poke each potato with a fork a few times and rub with oil. Place the potatoes on the middle or top rack in the oven and bake until cooked through, about 1 hour. (They should give a little when pressed.) Remove from the oven, but leave the oven on.

2. Meanwhile, heat a medium pan over medium heat. Generously coat the pan with oil. Add the ginger, garlic, jalapeño, and spices. Heat until fragrant, about 1 minute. Add the kale, cook for 4-5 minutes. Add a few

splashes of water if the kale starts to brown and stick to the pan.

3. When the potatoes are cool enough to handle, cut in half lengthwise, and scoop out the inside. Leave about ¼-inch of flesh on the potato.

4. In a bowl, mash the scooped out potato with the coconut milk. Stir in the kale.

5. Spoon the potato/kale mixture back into the potato halves.

6. Place the potato halves in a roasting pan and return to the oven to bake for another 15 minutes.

Serves 4-6

It is easier to scoop the flesh out of the potatoes if they are more round than oblong.

# Stuffed Cabbage Rolls

salt
olive oil for the pan
½ medium yellow onion, minced
2 medium stalks celery, ends trimmed, minced
½ medium red bell pepper, minced
3-4 cloves garlic, minced
1¼ cups gluten-free vegetable broth
⅓ cup brown basmati rice
⅓ cup brown lentils, picked through
2 teaspoons dried parsley
freshly ground black pepper
1 medium head green cabbage, cored
1 8-ounce can tomato sauce
1 6-ounce can tomato paste
½ cup water
⅓ cup red wine vinegar
½ teaspoon crushed red pepper

1. Fill a large pot with water, salt liberally, and bring to a boil.
2. Meanwhile, heat a large pan with a lid over medium-high heat. Lightly coat the pan with oil. Add the onion, celery, bell pepper, and garlic and sauté until the vegetables are soft and the onion is translucent, about 5 minutes.
3. Stir in the vegetable broth, rice, lentils, parsley, a pinch of salt and a few grinds of pepper. Cover and bring to a

boil. Reduce the heat to low and simmer for 60-75 minutes, until the broth is absorbed.

4. Once the water in the pot is boiling, gently lower the head of cabbage into the water. Cook a couple of minutes until the leaves are bright green and softened. Remove the outer leaves with tongs, setting them on a towel to dry. Continue cooking then removing leaves, until the entire cabbage is gently cooked.

5. Dump the water. Set the pot over low heat. Add the tomato sauce, tomato paste, water, red wine vinegar, and red pepper. Stir until well combined.

6. Take one cabbage leaf and spread it out on a cutting board. Cut out the center stem. Spread some lentil/rice filling a few inches from the uncut end of the leaf. While holding the cut sides overlapping, pick up the uncut end and roll over the filling. Fold in the sides. Continue until completely rolled. Place in the pot (seam-side down) on top of the tomato sauce. Repeat with the remaining leaves and filling.

7. Spoon some of the tomato sauce over the stuffed greens. Cover and increase the heat to medium-low. Simmer for 45-60 minutes.

Serves 4-6

It is important to completely remove the core from the head of cabbage. This is what allows the leaves to be easily removed from the boiling water.

# Vegan Sloppy Joes

*Sauce*
1 15-ounce can + 1 8-ounce can tomato sauce
1 8-ounce can tomato paste
¼ cup + 2 tablespoons molasses
1 tablespoon + 1 teaspoon apple cider vinegar
1 tablespoon liquid smoke
¾ teaspoon paprika
¼ rounded teaspoon crushed red pepper
¼ rounded teaspoon garlic powder
¼ rounded teaspoon ground cumin

*Filling*
1 14-ounce package extra firm tofu
olive oil for the pan
½ small yellow onion, diced
½ medium red bell pepper, diced
6 cloves garlic, minced
1 15-ounce can cannellini beans (approximately 1¾ cups), drained and rinsed

1. The night before, rinse and drain the tofu. Cut it into 8 even strips widthwise. Place in a covered container in the freezer.
2. In the morning, remove the tofu from the freezer and set it out to thaw. Once thawed, squeeze out any extra liquid and crumble it into pieces.

3. Place all of the sauce ingredients in a medium pot and stir to combine. Set over medium heat. Cook for 30 minutes, stirring occasionally.
4. For the filling, heat a large pan over medium heat. Lightly coat the pan with oil. Add the onion, bell pepper, and garlic. Sauté for 3-4 minutes, until the onion is softened and translucent.
5. Reduce the heat to low and add the tofu, beans, and sauce. Mash some of the beans using the back of a spoon. Stir well and cook until heated through, about 15 minutes. Serve on your favorite gluten-free buns.

Serves 6

Freezing then thawing the tofu gives it a chewier texture. While not a requirement, the tofu will freeze and thaw more quickly if placed in a single layer in the freezer. If the tofu isn't thawing quickly enough, run it under hot water or defrost it in the microwave. It is important to squeeze out any extra liquid to prevent the sauce from being watered down.

# Polenta Pie

½ cup julienned sun-dried tomatoes (not oil-packed)
½ cup hot water + approximately 2 cups water
½ medium yellow onion, diced
2 small zucchinis (⅔ pound), ends trimmed, cut into quarters lengthwise, then sliced into ⅛-inch pieces
½ teaspoon dried parsley
½ teaspoon dried sage
¼ teaspoon dried rosemary
¼ teaspoon dried thyme
pinch crushed red pepper
salt
1 cup finely ground polenta (cornmeal)
6 ounces shredded mozzarella cheese (optional)

1. Place sun-dried tomatoes in a bowl, and pour the ½ cup hot water over the tomatoes. Let stand.
2. Heat a medium pan over medium heat. Add the onion and sauté about 3 minutes, until softened. Add the zucchinis and cook 4-5 minutes. Drain the sun-dried tomatoes, but reserve the water. Add the tomatoes to the pan, stir into the vegetables, and remove from the heat.
3. Add enough water to the reserved tomato water to make 2½ cups. Place in a medium pot. Set on high heat and bring to a simmer. In a small bowl, mix the herbs, red pepper, and a large pinch of salt into the polenta. Once the water is simmering, reduce the heat to medium. Slowly stream in the polenta, while stirring to prevent

any lumps. Cook, stirring continuously, until the polenta is stiff enough to hold its shape. With finely ground polenta this should only take a few minutes; coarsely ground polenta will take longer. Stir the veggies into the polenta. Press into a 9-inch pie plate and refrigerate for 30 minutes.

4. Preheat the oven to 350°F. Remove the pie from the refrigerator and bake for 30 minutes. If using cheese, sprinkle over the pie and place under a broiler set on low for 5 minutes, until the cheese is melted.

Serves 4-8

# Fall Vegetable Terrine

½ 2-pound head cauliflower, leaves and stem removed, cut into 4 wedges
2 medium carrots (½ pound), ends trimmed, peeled
2 medium parsnips (½ pound), ends trimmed, peeled
1 medium Gala apple (½ pound), cored and quartered
extra virgin olive oil for drizzling and for the pan
1 small sweet potato (⅓ pound)
1¼ cups fresh cranberries
¼ cup water
1 tablespoon white sugar
1 teaspoon Dijon mustard
¼ pound Brussels sprouts, ends trimmed, diced
1 medium shallot, diced
salt
2 teaspoons prepared horseradish

1. Preheat the oven to 400°F. Grease a large baking sheet. Arrange the cauliflower, carrots, parsnips, and apple on the sheet, keeping each type of vegetable/fruit separate from the others. Lightly drizzle with oil, and toss to coat. Prick the sweet potato a few times with a knife. Place the sweet potato on the baking sheet, or directly on the oven rack if there is not enough room on the sheet.
2. Place the baking sheet in the oven and roast the vegetables/fruit for 45 minutes.
3. Meanwhile, combine the cranberries, water, sugar and mustard in a small pot. Set over medium heat. Cook un-

til the cranberries expand and then deflate, about 6-8 minutes. Mash some of the cranberries while cooking.

4. Heat a medium pan over medium heat. Lightly coat the pan with oil. Add the Brussels sprouts and shallot. Cook until beginning to brown, about 5 minutes.

5. Line an 8×5-inch loaf pan with plastic wrap. Remove the vegetables from the oven and let cool for a few minutes.

6. Add the parsnips, apple, a pinch of salt, and a drizzle of oil to a food processor. Pulse until a paste forms. Add the parsnip mix and Brussels sprouts/shallot to the loaf pan. Stir together and press into an even layer.

7. Add the cauliflower, horseradish, a pinch of salt, and a drizzle of oil to the food processor. Pulse until a paste forms. Spoon into a bowl.

8. Add the carrots, sweet potato (excluding the skin), a pinch of salt, and a drizzle of oil to the food processor. Pulse until a paste forms. Spoon into the loaf pan, and spread evenly. Cover with the cranberry mixture.

9. Spoon the cauliflower over the cranberries and smooth into an even layer. Wrap the edges of the plastic wrap over the terrine. Place in refrigerator, and allow to cool completely.

10. To serve, unwrap the top of the plastic wrap. Hold a serving dish over the top of the loaf pan, serving side down. Invert the two, so that the terrine now sits on the serving dish. Remove the plastic wrap.

Serves 8

# Enchiladas with Green Sauce

*Sauce*
olive oil for the baking sheet
3 poblano peppers
3 Anaheim peppers
¾ cup gluten-free vegetable broth
3 small tomatillos, cut into quarters
2-3 cloves garlic, peeled
½ teaspoon dried oregano
salt

*Enchiladas*
olive oil for the pan and casserole dish
½ medium white onion, minced
3-4 cloves garlic, minced
1 medium-large zucchini (¾ pound), ends trimmed, cut into ½-inch cubes
1 15-ounce can pinto beans (approximately 1¾ cups), drained and rinsed
12 5-inch gluten-free corn tortillas
3-4 ounces shredded queso fresco or Monterey jack

1. For the sauce, lightly grease a large baking sheet, and arrange the whole peppers on the sheet. Set an oven rack in the second highest position and set the broiler to low. Broil the peppers for 20-25 minutes, turning once or twice, until entirely blackened. Place the blackened peppers in a bowl, cover, and let steam for a few minutes.

Remove the skins (they should slip off) and cut out the stems and seeds.

2. Put the roasted peppers, vegetable broth, tomatillos, garlic, and oregano in a blender and process until smooth. Season to taste with salt. Pour into a bowl.

3. While the peppers are roasting, prepare the enchilada filling. Heat a large pan over medium heat. Lightly coat the pan with oil. Add the onion and garlic and cook for 3 minutes, until the onion is softened. Add the zucchini and cook for another 3-4 minutes, until softened. Add the beans and cook for 2 minutes, until heated through. Mash one-third of the beans with the back of the spoon. Remove from the heat.

4. Preheat the oven to 350°F. Grease a 9×13-inch casserole dish. Heat a medium pan over medium-low heat. Lightly coat the pan with oil. Place one tortilla in the pan and heat until softened, about 10-15 seconds per side. Lay on a flat surface and spoon the pepper sauce over both sides of the tortilla. Spoon the zucchini filling into the tortilla about one-third of the way from one edge. Roll and place seam-side down in the casserole dish. Repeat with remaining tortillas and filling. The pan will need to be lightly coated with more oil every 2-3 tortillas.

5. Once all the enchiladas have been rolled, cover with extra sauce, then sprinkle with cheese. Bake for 20-25 minutes, until bubbly.

Serves 4-6

# Tempeh Spinach Stuffed Peppers

¼ cup water
4 medium green or red bell peppers (2 pounds), stems, seeds, and ribs removed from the top
olive oil for the pan
8 ounces tempeh, crumbled
salt and freshly ground black pepper
1 medium yellow onion, diced
3 cloves garlic, minced
2 cups chopped baby spinach, well-packed (3 ounces)
1 cup cooked quinoa
1 teaspoon dried parsley
½ teaspoon dried rosemary
½ teaspoon crushed red pepper
1 8-ounce can tomato sauce, divided

1. Preheat the oven to 400°F.
2. Add the water to an 8×8-inch casserole dish. Place the peppers in, top side down. Bake for 15 minutes. Drain water from the dish (if there is any) and let the peppers cool.
3. Meanwhile, heat a large pan over medium-high heat. Lightly coat the pan with oil. Add the tempeh, a couple of pinches of salt, and a few grinds of pepper. Cook for about 5 minutes, until browned.

4. Push the tempeh over to one side of the pan and add the onion. Cook for a few minutes, until starting to brown around the edges. Push the onion to the side and add the garlic. Cook until fragrant, about 30 seconds.
5. Remove the pan from heat and stir in the spinach, quinoa, parsley, rosemary, red pepper, and half of the tomato sauce.
6. Stuff the peppers with the filling and return to the casserole dish. Top with the remaining tomato sauce.
7. Bake for 30 minutes, until the peppers are starting to wrinkle on top.

Serves 4

# Basic Vegetable Stir Fry

½ cup low-sodium gluten-free vegetable broth
¼ cup gluten-free soy sauce or tamari
2 teaspoons rice vinegar
2 teaspoons brown sugar
2 teaspoons cornstarch
few dashes toasted sesame seed oil
peanut or vegetable oil for the pan
2 large Napa cabbage leaves, cut into ¾-inch pieces
1 cup snow peas
½ small red bell pepper, cut into ¾-inch pieces
½ small green bell pepper, cut into ¾-inch pieces
1 cup medium broccoli florets
1 small carrot (2 ounces), ends trimmed, thinly sliced on a bias
½ small white onion, cut into ½-inch pieces
4-5 cloves garlic, minced
1½ cups canned vegetables (water chestnuts, bamboo shoots, baby corn, straw mushrooms)***

1. In a medium bowl, whisk together the vegetable broth, soy sauce or tamari, vinegar, sugar, cornstarch, and sesame seed oil.
2. Heat a large pan or wok over high heat. Lightly coat the pan with oil. Add the cabbage and snow peas. Cook, stirring occasionally, for 2-3 minutes, until lightly seared. Set aside in a medium bowl.

3. Add a little more oil. Add the bell peppers and cook, stirring occasionally, for 1½-2 minutes, until lightly seared. Set aside in the bowl.
4. Add a little more oil. Add the broccoli and carrots. Cook, stirring occasionally, for 2-3 minutes, until lightly seared. Set aside in the bowl.
5. Add a little more oil. Add the onion. Cook, stirring occasionally, for 1 minute, until lightly seared. Add the garlic. Cook until fragrant, about 30 seconds. Add the canned vegetables and all of the cooked vegetables back to the pan and stir to combine. Turn off the heat. Stir the sauce so that the cornstarch is mixed in, then add to the pan, and cook until thickened, about 30-60 seconds.

Serves 4

***Toss together one 8-ounce can of water chestnuts, one 8-ounce can of bamboo shoots, one 15-ounce can of baby corn, and one 15-ounce can of straw mushrooms. Divide the mixture evenly into thirds. Each third will be about 1½ cups. The extra can be frozen to be used next time.

Like any stir-fry this goes well over rice, but millet works nicely too.

# Eggless Broccoli Quiche

*Crust*
1⅓ cups water
⅔ cup millet
salt
2 tablespoons olive oil

*Quiche*
olive oil for the pan
1 medium yellow onion, diced
4 cloves garlic, diced
1½ blocks firm tofu, drained and rinsed
2 cups medium broccoli florets
½ medium red bell pepper, diced
½ cup nutritional yeast
½ teaspoon dried parsley
¼ teaspoon ground coriander
¼ teaspoon dried thyme
¼ teaspoon crushed red pepper
salt

1. For the crust, place the water, millet, and a pinch of salt in a small pot. Cover and bring to a boil. Reduce the heat to low and simmer for 20-30 minutes, until the water is absorbed. Remove from the heat, move the lid to partially uncover the pot, and let sit for 5 minutes.
2. Preheat the oven to 375°F. Combine 2 cups of the cooked millet, olive oil, and a pinch of salt in a food

processor. Process until a paste forms. Press into a 9-inch pie plate. Bake for 30 minutes.

3. For the quiche, heat a medium pan over medium heat. Lightly coat the pan with oil. Add the onion and garlic and cook 3-4 minutes, until pale yellow.

4. Pat the tofu dry and place in a large bowl. Mash into crumbles using a potato masher. Add the cooked onion and garlic mixture, broccoli, bell pepper, nutritional yeast, parsley, coriander, thyme, crushed red pepper, and a pinch of salt. Stir well.

5. Press the tofu mixture into the cooked crust. Return to the oven and bake for 30 minutes, until the top is lightly browned.

Serves 6-8

# Pasta e Fagioli
# (Pasta and Beans)

olive oil for the pot
½ medium yellow onion, diced
1 small carrot (2 ounces), ends trimmed, minced
1 small stalk celery, ends trimmed, minced
4 cloves garlic, minced
1 6-ounce can tomato paste
5 cups gluten-free vegetable broth
2 cups cooked cranberry beans
½ teaspoon dried parsley
¼ teaspoon dried rosemary
¼ teaspoon dried thyme
4 ounces short variety dried gluten-free pasta (e.g., fusilli, penne)
salt and freshly ground black pepper
shredded parmesan cheese (optional)

1. Heat a medium to large pot over medium heat. Lightly coat the bottom of the pot with oil. Add the onion, carrot, celery, and garlic and cook until soft, 5-7 minutes. Add in the tomato paste and cook about 5 minutes.

2. Add the broth, beans, and herbs. Scrape the bottom of the pot to loosen any bits of tomato paste. Increase the heat to high and bring the broth to a boil. Reduce the heat to medium, add the pasta, and cook until al dente, about 10 minutes. Season with salt and pepper to taste.

Ladle into bowls and garnish with parmesan cheese, if desired.

Serves 5-6

Cranberry beans are traditional for this dish, but I've only located them dried or fresh. If you would like to use canned beans, substitute kidney or pinto beans.

# Teriyaki Eggplant Steaks

⅓ cup mirin (or sake or dry white wine)
⅓ cup water
3 tablespoons gluten-free soy sauce or tamari
3-4 cloves garlic, minced
2 small scallions or green onions, minced
1 tablespoon minced ginger
pinch crushed red pepper
1 pound eggplant, stem removed, sliced into ¼-½ inch thick rounds
olive oil for the baking sheet

1. Combine everything except the eggplant in a small pot. Set over medium heat and simmer for about 10 minutes. The sauce will thicken slightly.
2. Lay the eggplant slices in a casserole dish or place in a large Ziploc plastic bag. Cover with the teriyaki sauce. Marinate for 1 hour, turning occasionally.
3. Preheat the oven to 350°F. Grease a large baking sheet. Remove the eggplant slices from the marinade and set in a single layer on the sheet. Bake for 45 minutes, turning once. In the last 5 minutes of cooking, return the marinade to the pot and set over medium heat. Let the marinade cook down to a thick sauce.
4. Plate the eggplant and spoon the marinade over the top.

Serves 4-6

If using sake or white wine, add 1 tablespoon of sugar or honey to the marinade.

# Aloo Gobi
# (Potatoes and Cauliflower)

3 cloves garlic, finely minced
1 tablespoon finely minced ginger
2 teaspoons ground coriander
½ teaspoon ground turmeric
¼ teaspoon crushed red pepper
1 tablespoon water
2 tablespoons peanut oil, or coconut oil, or ghee
1 teaspoon cumin seeds
1 teaspoon mustard seeds
2 cups small cauliflower florets
1 large Yukon Gold potato (¾ pound), cut into ½-inch cubes
1 15-ounce can tomato sauce
½ teaspoon salt

1. Place the garlic, ginger, coriander, turmeric, and red pepper in a small bowl and mix with the water to make a paste.
2. Heat a large pan with a lid over medium-high heat. Add the oil. Once the oil is shimmering, add the cumin and mustard seeds. Cover and cook until the seeds stop sputtering, 1-2 minutes.
3. Add the spice paste. Cook for 1-2 minutes until the mixture darkens and the spices begin to release their oils.
4. Add the cauliflower, potatoes, tomato sauce, and salt and stir well. Cover and reduce the heat to medium-low.

Cook for 40-45 minutes, stirring once or twice, until the potatoes and cauliflower are soft.

Serves 4

The seeds sputtering sounds like popcorn. It starts slow, speeds up, then sputters out.

# Zucchini and White Beans with Sage

olive oil for the pan
¼ cup well-packed fresh sage, cut into 1-inch sections
3 small zucchinis (1 pound), ends trimmed, sliced into
⅛-inch thick semicircles
2-3 cloves garlic, minced
2 15-ounce cans cannellini beans (approximately 3½
cups), drained and rinsed
zest of 1 medium lemon
salt and freshly ground black pepper

1. Heat a large pan over medium-high heat. Generously coat the pan with oil. Once the oil is hot, add the sage leaves and fry for 1-2 minutes, until the leaves are just beginning to brown. Set aside on a plate.

2. Reduce the heat to medium. Add the zucchini to the pan and cook about 5 minutes, until softened and yellow. Clear a spot in the pan, and add the garlic. Once fragrant, about 30 seconds, stir in the beans, lemon zest, and salt and pepper to taste. Cook for another 3-5 minutes, until heated through. Sprinkle sage leaves on top and serve.

Serves 4

# Pineapple Lime Glazed Tofu

2 12-ounce blocks extra firm tofu
1 12-ounce can frozen pineapple juice concentrate, thawed
½ cup + 2 tablespoons freshly squeezed lime juice
¼ cup white balsamic vinegar
¼ teaspoon crushed red pepper

1. Rinse the tofu and pat dry. Place between towels on a flat surface. Place something flat (e.g., a cutting board) over the top and set some weight (e.g., a couple cans of beans) on top of that. Let sit for 30 minutes to press out excess water. Cut each drained tofu block into 8 slices widthwise.

2. Whisk the remaining ingredients in a large casserole dish. Heat a large pan or griddle over medium heat. Cook the tofu slices 1½-2 minutes per side, until golden. Place in the marinade and let sit for 1 hour.

3. Heat the same pan over medium heat. Working in batches, cook the tofu, about 2 minutes per side, while spooning some of the marinade over the pieces. The marinade will cook down to a thick glaze. If it becomes too thick and sticky, just add a little more marinade.

Serves 4-6

The tofu can be marinated overnight, and then the recipe can be continued from Step 3.

# Millet Tabbouli

¾ cup millet
1½ cups water
salt
⅔ cup finely chopped fresh parsley
¼ cup finely chopped fresh mint
1 medium tomato (½ pound), seeds removed, diced
1 small English cucumber (⅔ pound), seeds removed, diced
¼ cup extra virgin olive oil
¼ cup freshly squeezed lemon juice
3-4 cloves garlic, finely minced

1. Place the millet in a medium pot over medium heat. Toast for a few minutes while shaking the pot. The millet will brown slightly and smell nutty. Add the water and a few pinches of salt. Increase the heat to high, cover, and bring to a boil. Reduce the heat to low and simmer for 20-30 minutes. Once the water is absorbed, remove from the heat, fluff, and let cool.

2. In a large bowl, stir together the cooked millet, parsley, mint, tomato, and cucumber. In a small bowl, whisk together the olive oil, lemon juice, garlic, and salt to taste. Pour over the millet mixture, and stir well.

Serves 4-6

This recipe can be made with half the oil and lemon juice, but I prefer the fuller flavor of more.

English cucumbers have thinner skin than standard cucumbers, so they are generally sold wrapped in plastic.

# Mushrooms in Balsamic Glaze over Sautéed Spinach

½ cup julienned sundried tomatoes (not oil-packed)
¾ cup hot water
olive oil for the pan
1 pound crimini mushrooms, sliced
salt and freshly ground black pepper
½ cup balsamic vinegar
¼ cup water
½ teaspoon dried parsley
½ teaspoon dried thyme
4 cloves garlic, minced
1 medium shallot, minced
10 ounces baby spinach

1. Place the tomatoes in a bowl and cover with the hot water. Let sit.
2. Heat a large pan over medium heat. Lightly coat the pan with oil. Add the mushrooms, a pinch of salt, and a couple of grinds of pepper, and stir well. Cook, stirring occasionally, until the mushrooms have released all of their juice and the juice has cooked off, about 10-12 minutes.
3. Add the vinegar, water, parsley, and thyme to the mushrooms. Stir, and allow the liquids to reduce until the pan is mostly dry, 10-12 minutes.

4. When the liquid in the mushroom pan is reduced by half, about 5-6 minutes, heat another large pan over medium-high heat. Drain the tomatoes. Lightly coat the pan with oil. Add the garlic, shallot, and tomatoes. Cook until fragrant, about 1 minute. Start adding the spinach in batches, stirring well between each addition to allow the spinach to wilt. Continue until all the spinach is wilted, about 3-4 minutes. Season to taste with salt and pepper.

5. To serve, divide the spinach and tomatoes between 4 plates, then top with the mushrooms.

Serves 4

# Apple Potato Tempeh Hand Pies

*Dough*
⅔ cup sorghum flour
2 tablespoons brown rice flour
½ cup tapioca starch
1½ teaspoons white sugar
½ teaspoon xanthan gum
½ teaspoon salt
8 tablespoons cold butter (1 stick), cut in large chunks
approximately ¼ cup cold water
1 large egg (optional)
3 tablespoons water (optional)

*Filling*
4 ounces tempeh, diced
1 large stalk celery, ends trimmed, diced
1 small Granny Smith apple (⅓ pound), cut into ½-inch cubes
1 small Yukon Gold potato (¼ pound), cut into ½-inch cubes
½ small yellow onion, diced
salt and freshly ground black pepper

1. For the crust, whisk together the flours, starch, sugar, xanthan gum, and salt in a medium bowl. Lay out a sheet of plastic wrap nearby. Place the flour mixture and butter in the bowl of a food processor. Pulse until the

butter is incorporated but still fairly large in size. Slowly pour the water through the feed tube while pulsing. Stop once the dough looks crumbly and the butter is pea-sized. (More than ¼ cup of water may be needed, but try to use as little as possible, adding just a little at a time.)

2. Turn the dough out onto the plastic wrap. Gather up the sides and press the dough into a large ball. Divide the dough into four even pieces and form into disks. Wrap each in plastic wrap and place in the refrigerator for 30 minutes.

3. Meanwhile, stir all of the filling ingredients together in a large bowl. Season generously with salt and pepper.

4. Preheat the oven to 350°F. Line a large baking sheet with parchment paper. If using, beat the egg and water together in a small bowl to make an egg wash.

5. Lay out a large sheet of plastic wrap. Dust liberally with brown rice flour. Place one of the disks in the middle of the flour. Sprinkle more flour on top, and cover with another sheet of plastic wrap. Roll out the dough, stopping to add more flour a few times, until it's a rough circle around ¼-inch thick. Remove the top sheet of plastic wrap. Hold the rolling pin close to the edge of the dough. Lift the nearest edge of the plastic wrap up and over the rolling pin, so that the dough drapes over the rolling pin. Pull the plastic wrap away from the dough. Transfer the dough to the parchment-lined baking sheet.

6. Spoon one-fourth of the filling mixture onto half of the circle, leaving about one inch around the edge. If using the egg wash, brush around the edge with a pastry brush. Fold the unfilled half over the filled half until the edges meet. Starting on one side, pinch the edges together, and crimp upwards. Repeat with remaining three pieces of dough. Brush any remaining egg wash over the hand pies, if using.

7. Bake for 1 hour, until the pies are lightly browned. If using the egg wash, the pies will be more golden-brown.

Serves 4

It's not required to use the egg wash to seal the hand pies, but it makes them seal much better.

# Buckwheat Pilaf

1 small carnival or acorn squash (1-1¼ pound), peeled,
seeds removed, cut into ½-inch cubes
olive oil for drizzling and frying
¼ cup fresh sage leaves, cut into 1-inch sections
½ medium yellow onion, diced
¾ cup toasted buckwheat groats (kasha)
2 cups gluten-free vegetable broth
pinch or two of saffron

1. Preheat the oven to 400°F. Place the squash on a medium baking sheet. Lightly drizzle with oil, and toss to coat. Bake for 30 minutes.

2. Meanwhile, heat a large pan with a lid over medium-high heat. Generously coat the pan with oil. Add the sage leaves. Fry for 1-1½ minutes, until the edges of the leaves are darkened and the sage is crispy. Set aside on a plate.

3. Reduce the heat to medium. Add the onion and sauté for 3 minutes, until softened. Add the buckwheat groats and cook for 5 minutes, until lightly browned. Add the vegetable broth and saffron. Cover and bring to a boil. Reduce the heat to low and simmer for around 30 minutes, until all liquid is absorbed. Add the cooked squash. Cover and let sit 5 minutes. Stir to incorporate the squash. Garnish with fried sage and serve.

Serves 4-6

# Lentil Crepes with Cauliflower and Peas

*Lentil Crepes*
½ cup red lentils, picked through
½ cup Arborio rice
1¼ cups water
salt
coconut oil or olive oil for the pan

*Filling*
2 tablespoons coconut oil or olive oil + more for the pan
½ medium yellow onion, diced
2 cups medium cauliflower florets
1 cup frozen peas
salt
¼ cup water
¼ cup finely shredded unsweetened coconut
1 tablespoon minced ginger
¾ teaspoon dry mustard powder
¾ teaspoon ground coriander
½ teaspoon ground turmeric
¼ teaspoon crushed red pepper

1. For the crepes, place the lentils and rice in a medium bowl and cover with cool water. Let sit for 30 minutes.
2. After 30 minutes, drain off the water and rinse the lentils and rice. Place in a blender and add the 1¼ cups wa-

ter and a large pinch of salt. Blend until a thin batter forms.

3. Preheat the oven to 200°F. Heat a large pan over medium heat. Lightly coat the pan with oil. Spread a large spoonful of batter into the pan in a circular motion and swirl the pan to spread the batter into an even 6-8 inch circle. Cook 1-1½ minutes, until the edges start to lift from the pan. Flip and cook another 45-60 seconds. Remove from the pan and set on a large oven-safe dish. Continue with the remaining batter. Add a little more oil to the pan every few crepes. Place in the oven to keep warm.

4. For the filling, heat a large pan with a lid over medium heat. Lightly coat the pan with oil. Add the onion and cook for 3 minutes, until softened. Stir in the cauliflower, peas, and a large pinch of salt. Add the water, cover, and let steam for 7-8 minutes, until the cauliflower is softened with a little bite.

5. Meanwhile, heat a medium pan over medium heat. Add the 2 tablespoons oil, and stir in the coconut and ginger. Cook until the coconut starts to darken, about 2 minutes. Add the spices and cook another 30-60 seconds.

6. Add the coconut/spice mixture to the cauliflower and stir to combine. Serve with the crepes.

Makes approximately 8 crepes

# Bell Pepper Portobello Fajitas and Fresh Corn Tortillas

*Fajita Marinade*
3 tablespoons freshly squeezed lime juice
2 tablespoons tequila
2 tablespoons olive oil
3-4 cloves garlic, finely minced
1 large jalapeño pepper, stem and seeds removed, finely minced
¼ cup chopped fresh cilantro
½ teaspoon ground cumin
salt

*Fajitas*
2 small green or red bell peppers (¾ pound), sliced
2 large portobello mushrooms, sliced
½ medium white onion, sliced root to stem
olive oil for the pan
8 corn tortillas (see below)

1. In a small bowl, mix all of the marinade ingredients together, seasoning with salt to taste. Place in a large casserole dish or Ziploc plastic bag. Add the bell peppers, mushrooms, and onion. Toss to coat. Let marinate for 1 hour, mixing once or twice.
2. Heat a large heavy-bottomed pan over high heat. Generously coat the pan with oil. Add the marinated vegetables, draining as much of the marinade away as possible.

3. Cook, stirring infrequently, until marinade has cooked off and the vegetables are starting to sear at the edges, 5-7 minutes. Serve immediately with warmed tortillas.

Serves 4

*Fresh Corn Tortillas*
1 cup masa harina
salt
⅔-1 cup warm water

1. Mix the masa harina and a couple of pinches of salt in a mixing bowl. Add ⅔ cup water. Stir until dough forms. If that is not enough liquid to form dough, add a little more water. Knead a few times and form into a ball. Cover and let rest for 15 minutes.
2. Divide the dough into 8 pieces. Roll into balls. Smash a piece between two sheets of parchment paper, by pressing firmly with the bottom of a dinner plate. Roll the tortillas out to 6-7 inches. Alternatively, press each dough ball between two sheets of parchment paper using a tortilla press. Repeat with the remaining balls of dough.
3. Heat a pan over medium-high heat. Place one tortilla in the pan. Cook about 1½ minutes, until brown spots appear. Flip and cook the other side for 1½ minutes. Place in a towel to keep warm. Repeat with remaining tortillas.

Makes 8

Make the tortillas while the vegetables marinate. Roll from the center of the tortilla, not quite all the way to the edge. It's important to keep them warm in the towel so they stay pliable.

Depending on the size of the pan, the filling may need to be cooked in batches so that the pan is not crowded. A crowded pan prevents good searing.

Masa harina is a special kind of corn flour frequently used in Mexican cuisine. Look for it in the Mexican food section of your grocery store.

# Stinky Macaroni and Cheese

8 ounces short variety dried gluten-free pasta (e.g., fusilli, penne, macaroni)
3 tablespoons butter
2 tablespoons white rice flour
1 tablespoon potato starch
1 cup gluten-free vegetable broth
½ cup gluten-free hard pear cider or dry white wine
4 ounces gluten-free blue cheese, crumbled
2 ounces shredded Gruyère cheese
2 ounces shredded asiago cheese
freshly ground black pepper

1. Bring a medium to large pot of water to boil. Add the pasta and cook until al dente, 10-12 minutes. Drain.
2. Meanwhile, once the water is near boiling, melt the butter in a large pan over medium-low heat. Whisk in the flour and starch. Cook for 5 minutes, until golden.
3. Add the vegetable broth and cider or wine. Increase the heat to medium. Simmer, while whisking frequently, for 4-5 minutes, until the mixture thickens.
4. Stir in the cheeses until the sauce is smooth, around 2 minutes. Season with black pepper to taste. Stir the noodles into the cheese sauce.

Serves 4

# Mushroom Nut Roast

olive oil for the pans
1 medium yellow onion, diced
1 medium stalk celery, ends trimmed, diced
3-4 cloves garlic, minced
1 pound crimini mushrooms, cut into ½-inch cubes
½ cup white wine or gluten-free vegetable broth
salt
2 cups pecans
1 cup walnuts
1 cup fresh gluten-free bread crumbs
1 teaspoon dried parsley
1 teaspoon dried sage
½ teaspoon dried thyme
½ teaspoon dried oregano
freshly ground black pepper
2 large eggs

1. Preheat the oven to 375°F. Grease a 9×5-inch loaf pan and line it with parchment paper.
2. Heat a medium to large pan over medium heat. Lightly coat the pan with oil. Add the onion and celery. Cook, stirring occasionally, for 5 minutes, until the onion is translucent and just beginning to brown.
3. Clear a spot in the pan and add the garlic. Cook until fragrant, 30 seconds. Add the mushrooms, wine or broth, and a pinch of salt. Stir well. Increase the heat to medium-high. Allow the mushrooms to release their

juices. Continue to cook until most, but not all of the liquid has cooked off, about 10 minutes.

4. Meanwhile, pulse the nuts in a food processor until evenly ground, but not a fine powder. Place in a large mixing bowl with the bread crumbs. Stir in the herbs, a pinch of salt, and a few grinds of pepper.

5. Add the cooked mushrooms to the mixing bowl and stir well. Lightly beat the eggs in a small bowl, and then stir into the nut mixture.

6. Spoon the mixture into the prepared loaf pan, firmly press it down, and smooth the top.

7. Bake for 45 minutes, until the edges are browned and a toothpick inserted in the loaf comes out clean. Remove from the oven and let cool slightly. Run a knife around the edges if necessary. Place a serving platter over the loaf pan, serving-side down. Invert the two together. Remove the parchment paper and serve.

Serves 8

# Collard Green Wraps

salt
4 large collard green leaves
½ cup water
3 ounces dried apricots, minced
2 tablespoons Dijon mustard
¼ teaspoon crushed red pepper
olive oil for the pan
4 ounces tempeh, stood on side and cut in half, then
cut into fourths lengthwise (8 pieces)
2 ounces sprouts
2 ounces gluten-free blue cheese, crumbled

1. Fill a medium pot with water, salt liberally, and bring to a boil. Add one of the leaves and simmer for around 1 minute, until bright green. Remove and set on a towel to dry. Repeat with the remaining leaves.

2. In a small pot, mix the water, apricots, mustard, and red pepper. Bring to a simmer, cover, and cook for 15 minutes. Remove the lid and let cool.

3. Meanwhile, heat a medium pan over medium heat. Lightly coat the pan with oil, then add the tempeh. Cook around 2 minutes, flip, then cook another 2 minutes, until lightly browned.

4. To assemble, cut the stem out of each leaf, about two-thirds of the way through the leaf. Lay flat and cross over the cut ends of the leaf, to form a continuous surface. Spoon one-fourth of the apricot mixture onto the

uncut end of the leaf. Lay two pieces of tempeh on the apricots. Cover with one-fourth of the sprouts and one-fourth of the cheese. Taking care to hold the cut ends overlapping each other, pick up the uncut end of the leaf, and roll over the filling. Fold in both sides. Continue until completely rolled. Repeat with remaining leaves and filling.

Serves 4

# Summery Wild Rice Salad

2 cups gluten-free vegetable broth
2 cups water
⅔ cup wild rice
½ teaspoon dried rosemary, crushed
1 bay leaf
½ large yellow onion, sliced root to stem
1 teaspoon olive oil
1 large peach (½ pound), diced
1 cup Bing cherries, pitted and cut into quarters
1 cup chopped curly endive/frisée
1½ tablespoons freshly squeezed lemon juice
salt and freshly ground black pepper

1. Place the broth, water, rice, rosemary, and bay leaf in a medium pot. Set over high heat, cover, and bring to a boil. Reduce the heat to medium, and simmer for 1-1¼ hours, until the rice is opened and tender. Remove the bay leaf. Drain any remaining liquid. Place rice in a large bowl and let cool to room temperature.

2. Meanwhile, heat a medium pan over medium heat. Add the onion and cook, stirring occasionally, for 5 minutes. Add the olive oil and reduce the heat to just under medium. Cook, stirring frequently, for around 15 minutes, until the onion is brown and frizzled.

3. Stir the onion, peach, cherries, endive, and lemon juice into the cooled rice. Season with salt and pepper to taste.

Serves 4-6

The amount of time it takes to cook the frizzled onion varies quite a bit. Keep an eye on it. Stirring frequently, especially once the onion starts to brown, helps to prevent burning.

# Stovetop Eggplant Parmesan

1 pound eggplant, stem removed, sliced ¼-inch thick
salt
olive oil for the pots
½ medium yellow onion, minced
2-3 cloves garlic, minced
1 28-ounce can crushed tomatoes
1 teaspoon dried basil
½ teaspoon dried parsley
¼ teaspoon dried oregano
¼ teaspoon crushed red pepper
2 eggs, beaten
½ cup finely ground dried gluten-free bread crumbs
4 ounces shredded parmesan cheese

1. Set the eggplant in a colander or on a cooling rack in the sink. Sprinkle each side liberally with salt and let sit for 30 minutes to draw moisture out of the eggplant.
2. Meanwhile, heat a medium pot over medium heat. Lightly coat the bottom of the pot with oil. Add the onion and garlic and sauté for a few minutes. Add the tomatoes, basil, parsley, oregano, and crushed red pepper. Stir well, cover, reduce the heat to low, and let it simmer while you prepare the eggplant.
3. Thoroughly rinse the eggplant slices and pat dry. Set out a shallow, wide bowl with the eggs, and a shallow, wide bowl with the bread crumbs. Set a large pan or pot with a lid over medium heat, and lightly coat it with oil. Indi-

vidually coat a piece of eggplant in egg, then in bread-crumbs and set in the pan. Add as many slices of egg-plant as will fit. Cook for 2-3 minutes until the bottoms are browned, then flip and cook another 2-3 minutes. Remove the eggplant and wipe out the pan. Repeat the process with the remaining eggplant slices, until all have been breaded and fried. Wipe out the pan.

4. Set the pan over low heat. Carefully add the eggplant slices, in one overlapping layer, starting around the edge of the pan and working inwards. Top with tomato sauce. Cover and cook for 30 minutes.

5. Remove the lid and sprinkle the cheese over the top. Cook for another 5-10 minutes, until the cheese is melt-ed.

Serves 4-6

Since the pan is thoroughly preheated, it may take the 2$^{nd}$ and 3$^{rd}$ batches of eggplants less time to cook and/or you may need to lower the heat.

# Baked Pasta with Collard Greens and Squash

olive oil for the casserole dish and pan
1 small acorn squash (1-1¼ pound), cut in half, seeds removed
salt
6 ounces short variety dried gluten-free pasta (e.g., fusilli, penne)
10 cloves garlic, thinly sliced
1 large red bell pepper (¾ pound), cut into ½-inch pieces
½ pound collard greens, stems removed and chopped (about 3 cups)
¼ cup pine nuts
3 tablespoons chopped fresh parsley
½ teaspoon smoked paprika
1 cup shredded Gruyère cheese

1. Preheat the oven to 400°F. Grease an 8×8-inch casserole dish and arrange the squash cut side down. Roast for 30 minutes. Remove from the oven and let cool. Reduce the oven temperature to 350°F.
2. Bring a medium to large pot of water to a boil and salt liberally. Meanwhile, score the inside of the squash into sections about ½-inch square and scoop out the flesh.
3. Add the pasta to the boiling water. Heat a large pan over medium-high heat. Lightly coat the pan with oil. Add

the garlic and bell pepper, and cook for a couple of minutes. Add the collard greens and cook until softened, about 5 minutes. Add a couple of splashes of water if the greens stick to the pan. Remove the pan from heat.

4. Drain the noodles while still slightly crunchy, about 8 minutes. Add the noodles, squash, pine nuts, parsley, paprika, and a pinch of salt to the pan. Stir well.

5. Spread one-third of the pasta mixture in an 8x8-inch casserole dish. Sprinkle with one-third of the cheese. Layer on another one-third of the pasta, followed by another layer of cheese, then the rest of the pasta, and a final layer of cheese. Bake for 25-30 minutes.

Serves 4-6

# Lentils with Olive Salad over Polenta

*Lentils*
olive oil for the pot
¼ bulb fennel, white part only, minced
1 large shallot, minced
1 cup gluten-free vegetable broth
⅓ cup beluga lentils, picked through
zest of 1 small orange
1 bay leaf

*Polenta*
1½ cups water or gluten-free vegetable broth
1 cup unsweetened soymilk
pinch ground cayenne pepper
salt and freshly ground black pepper
½ cup finely ground polenta (cornmeal)

*Olive Topping*
3-4 Greek black olives, diced
3-4 green olives, diced
3-4 Castelvetrano olives, diced
2 tablespoons diced roasted red pepper

1. For the lentils, heat a small to medium pot over medium-low heat, and lightly coat the bottom of the pot with oil. Add the fennel and shallot and cook for 10 minutes, until beginning to brown. Add the vegetable

broth, lentils, zest, and bay leaf. Increase the heat to high, cover, and bring to a boil. Reduce the heat to low and simmer for 1 hour.

2. When the lentils are nearly ready, start the polenta. Heat the water or vegetable broth and milk in a medium to large pot over medium heat. Once simmering, reduce the heat to medium-low, and add cayenne, a pinch or two of salt (more if using water), and a few grinds of pepper. Slowly stream in the polenta while whisking to prevent lumps. Cook while stirring occasionally, until all of the liquid is absorbed and the polenta is creamy and smooth. With finely ground polenta this should only take a few minutes; coarsely ground polenta will take longer.

3. Drain any remaining liquid from the lentils. For the olive topping, stir the olives and roasted red peppers together in a small bowl.

4. To serve, spoon the polenta into the bottom of a serving dish. Spoon the lentils over the polenta, then top with the olive mix.

Serves 4

I use beluga lentils because they retain their shape and don't get mushy when cooked. Standard brown lentils won't work nearly as well.

# Not Shepherd's Pie

2 large russet potatoes (1½ pounds), cubed
salt
2 tablespoons olive oil + more for the pan
2 small carrots (¼ pound), ends trimmed, cut into ½-inch cubes
1 large stalk celery, ends trimmed, cut into ½-inch pieces
½ medium yellow onion, cut into ½-inch pieces
½ pound crimini mushrooms, cut into ½-inch cubes
1 15-ounce can of chickpeas, drained and rinsed
1 teaspoon dried parsley
½ teaspoon dried sage
½ teaspoon dried rosemary
½ teaspoon ground cumin
2 tablespoons tapioca starch
¾ cup gluten-free mushroom or vegetable broth
1 tablespoon dry mustard powder
1 teaspoon gluten-free soy sauce or tamari
½ cup unsweetened soymilk
freshly ground black pepper

1. Put the potatoes in a medium pot. Cover with cold water and add a large pinch of salt. Cover and bring to a boil. Reduce the heat to low and simmer for 15-20 minutes, until the potatoes are soft.

2. Meanwhile, heat a large pan over medium heat. Lightly coat the pan with oil. Add the carrots, celery, and onion and sauté for 5 minutes. Add the mushrooms and sea-

son with a couple of large pinches of salt. Allow the juices to cook out, 4-5 minutes. Add the chickpeas, parsley, sage, rosemary, cumin, and starch. Stir well. Lightly mash some of the chickpeas with the back of a spoon. Add the mushroom or vegetable broth, mustard, and soy sauce or tamari. Cook while stirring until the sauce thickens, a few minutes.

3. Drain the potatoes. Mash with the milk and 2 tablespoons of olive oil. Season with salt and pepper to taste.

4. Place the chickpea filling in a 9-inch pie pan or 8×8-inch casserole dish. Spread the mashed potatoes to cover the top. Use a fork to make ridges in the potatoes.

5. Set the oven broiler to low. Place the dish on the second rack under the broiler. Broil for 8-12 minutes, until the potatoes are golden-brown.

Serves 4-6

# Ricotta Gnocchi
# in Vodka Sauce

*Vodka Sauce*
olive oil for the pan
1 small carrot (2 ounces), ends trimmed, minced
1 small stalk celery, ends trimmed, minced
½ medium yellow onion, minced
4 cloves garlic, minced
1 15-ounce can tomato puree
¼ cup vodka
¼ cup whipping cream

*Gnocchi*
½ cup sorghum flour
¼ cup brown rice flour
¼ cup tapioca starch
scant ¼ teaspoon ground nutmeg
salt and freshly ground black pepper
16 ounces ricotta cheese

1. For the vodka sauce, set a large pan over medium heat. Lightly coat the pan with oil. Add the carrot, celery, onion, and garlic. Cook until softened, about 3 minutes. Add the tomato puree. When it begins to bubble, reduce the heat to low and simmer for 20-30 minutes.

2. Meanwhile, start the gnocchi. Stir the flours, starch, nutmeg, a pinch of salt, and a few grinds of pepper together in a large bowl. Mix in the ricotta until fully in-

corporated. Flour a large work surface. Gently roll the dough into cylinders about ½-inch across. Cut into ½-inch segments.

3. After the sauce has simmered 20-30 minutes, interrupt the gnocchi making to puree the sauce in a blender or food processor. Return to the pan and stir in the vodka. Simmer the sauce for another 20-30 minutes.

4. Set a medium to large pot of water to boil. Resume rolling out the gnocchi. Once all the gnocchi have been rolled and the pot is boiling, salt the water and reduce it to a gentle simmer.

5. Stir the cream into the vodka tomato sauce.

6. Add the gnocchi to the water in batches. Once each batch of gnocchi floats to the top, count to 10, then remove them with a slotted spoon. Place them in a colander set over a bowl. After all the gnocchi have been cooked, gently stir them into the sauce and serve.

Serves 4-6

Make sure to keep re-flouring the work surface while rolling out the gnocchi. It is also helpful to wipe any excess dough off of the knife used to cut the gnocchi. This makes it easier to get a clean cut.

# Cabbage Kidney Bean Casserole

olive oil for the pan
1 medium yellow onion, diced
1 small bulb fennel, white part only, cut in half, thinly sliced
1 pound green cabbage, thinly sliced
salt
4 tablespoons butter (½ stick)
2 tablespoons sorghum flour
2 tablespoons tapioca starch
1½ cups gluten-free vegetable broth
2 tablespoons Dijon mustard
2 15-ounce cans kidney beans (approximately 3½ cups), drained and rinsed
½ teaspoon dried parsley
¼ teaspoon crushed red pepper
2 ounces shredded gouda cheese
1 cup fresh gluten-free bread crumbs

1. Preheat the oven to 350°F. Heat a large, oven-safe pan over medium heat and lightly coat with oil. Add the onion and fennel and cook until softened, 5 minutes. Add the cabbage and a large pinch of salt. Cook until the cabbage is wilted and beginning to brown around the edges, 5-10 minutes.

2. Meanwhile, melt the butter in a small pot over medium heat. Whisk together the flour and starch, and then add

to the butter, whisking thoroughly. Cook, whisking fre-quently, until the flours are golden-brown, 5-10 minutes.

3. Slowly pour the vegetable broth in the pot, whisking continuously. Whisk in the mustard. Cook as it thick-ens, until a finger drawn over the back of the spoon leaves a clean line, 3-4 minutes. Remove from the heat.

4. Add the kidney beans, parsley, red pepper, and sauce to the cabbage. Stir well. Stir in the cheese. Smooth the top and coat with bread crumbs. Bake for 45 minutes, until the bread crumbs are golden-brown.

Serves 8

I like making this dish with smoked gouda, but regular gouda is good too. I typically use a baguette to make the bread crumbs, but sandwich bread works just fine. A cast iron pan is perfect for transitioning from the stovetop to the oven.

# Pesto Asparagus Galette

*Crust*
½ cup + 2 tablespoons tapioca starch
¼ cup white rice flour
¼ cup buckwheat flour
2 tablespoons dry milk powder
2 teaspoons white sugar
½ teaspoon xanthan gum
½ teaspoon salt
8 tablespoons cold butter (1 stick), cut into large chunks
¼ cup cold water

*Filling*
¾ cup well-packed fresh basil
3 tablespoons pine nuts
2 teaspoons extra virgin olive oil
1 teaspoon freshly squeezed lemon juice
salt and freshly ground black pepper
¼ pound asparagus, cut into ¼-inch pieces
1 small leek, white and light green parts only, thinly sliced

1. For the crust, whisk together the starch, flours, milk powder, sugar, xanthan gum, and salt in a medium bowl. Lay out a sheet of plastic wrap nearby. Add the flour mixture and butter to the bowl of a food processor. Pulse until the butter is incorporated but still fairly large in size. Slowly pour the water through the feed tube

while pulsing. Stop once the dough looks crumbly and the butter is pea-sized.

2. Turn the mixture out onto the plastic wrap. Gather up the sides of the wrap and press the dough into a ball. Flatten the dough into a disk, wrap in the plastic wrap, and refrigerate for 20 minutes.

3. For the filling, clean out the food processor, and add the basil, pine nuts, olive oil, lemon juice, a few large pinches of salt, and a couple grinds of pepper. Pulse until a chunky paste forms. In a medium bowl, stir the pesto with the asparagus and leek.

4. Preheat the oven to 400°F. Line a large baking sheet with parchment paper. Lay out two large overlapping sheets of plastic wrap. Dust the plastic wrap with white rice flour. Have extra sheets ready to lay on top of the dough.

5. Put the chilled dough on the floured plastic wrap. Sprinkle flour over the top of the dough, and then lay two sheets of plastic wrap over the top. Roll out the dough, stopping to add more flour a few times, until it is a rough circle between ⅛ and ¼-inch thick. Remove the top sheets of plastic wrap. Hold the rolling pin close to the edge of the dough. Lift the nearest edge of the plastic wrap up and over the rolling pin, so that the dough drapes over the rolling pin. Pull the plastic wrap away from the dough. Transfer the dough to the parchment-lined baking sheet.

6. Spread the asparagus/leek mixture on the dough, leaving about one inch around the edges. Gently fold over the edges of the dough, to make a crust. Bake for 30 minutes, until the crust is golden-brown.

Serves 4

I use two sheets of overlapping plastic wrap to ensure I have enough space to roll out the dough. If the dough starts to crack while rolling out, simply lift the plastic wrap and press the two sections together. You can also press little crumbs from around the edges back into the dough.

# Vegetarian "Chicken" Salad

2 15-ounce cans chickpeas (about 3 cups), drained
and rinsed
1 large stalk celery, ends trimmed, diced
½ small red onion, diced
¼ cup mayonnaise or Vegenaise
3 tablespoons dill relish
3 tablespoons Dijon mustard
salt and freshly ground black pepper

1. Place the chickpeas in a large bowl. Mash about half of
   them.
2. Stir in the celery and onion. Add the mayonnaise or
   Vegenaise, relish, and mustard. Mix well. Season to taste
   with salt and pepper. Eat plain or serve on your favorite
   gluten-free sandwich bread.

Serves 4-6

# Drunken Spaghetti

salt
½ ounce dried porcini mushrooms
2 tablespoons extra virgin olive oil, divided
2 tablespoons butter, divided
¼ pound crimini mushrooms, minced
2 medium shallots, minced
½ head garlic, minced
2 cups dry red wine
8 ounces dried gluten-free spaghetti noodles
shredded parmesan cheese (optional)

1. Bring a large pot of salted water to a boil. Meanwhile, place the porcini mushrooms in a small bowl, cover with hot water, and let sit 10 minutes. Drain and rinse under running water to wash away any grit. Mince.

2. Heat a large pan over medium heat. Add 1 tablespoon each of olive oil and butter. Once melted, add the porcini and crimini mushrooms, shallots, and garlic and cook for 5 minutes. Add the wine to the pan.

3. Add the noodles to the boiling water. Let the noodles cook until limp, but still firm in the middle, around 8 minutes. Transfer the noodles to the pan, and cook until most of the wine is absorbed and the noodles are fully cooked, about 5 minutes. If the pan gets too dry, add a couple spoonfuls of pasta water. Turn off the heat and

stir in the remaining butter and olive oil. Garnish with parmesan cheese, if desired.

Serves 4

# Steamed Veggies
# in Peanut Sauce

1½ cups large broccoli florets
1 medium red bell pepper, cut into ¾-inch pieces
1 cup snow peas, cut in half
1 cup pineapple cut into ½-inch chunks (1 8-ounce can)
1 cup cut baby corn (1 8-ounce can)
olive oil for the pot
4 cloves garlic, minced
1 serrano pepper, stem and seeds removed, minced
¾ cup full-fat canned coconut milk
½ cup peanut butter
3 tablespoons gluten-free soy sauce or tamari

1. Put about ½ inch of water in a medium pot. Fit a steamer basket in the pot. Cover and place over high heat. Once boiling, add the broccoli and let steam for 3 minutes. Add the bell pepper and snow peas and steam for another 3 minutes. Add the pineapple and baby corn and steam another 3 minutes. Remove the steaming basket from the pot, then drain.

2. Meanwhile, heat a small pot over medium heat. Lightly coat the bottom of the pot with oil. Add the garlic and serrano pepper and cook for 30 seconds, until fragrant. Add the coconut milk, peanut butter, and soy sauce or tamari. Reduce the heat to low and whisk until thick-

ened, about 5 minutes. Plate the steamed veggies and cover with the peanut sauce.

Serves 4

# Millet Tempeh Walnut "Meatballs"

⅔ cup water
⅓ cup millet
olive oil for the pan
1 large shallot, diced
½ medium red bell pepper, diced
2 ounces tempeh, diced
½ cup walnuts
1 teaspoon dried basil
1 teaspoon dried parsley
½ teaspoon dried oregano
1½ ounces grated parmesan cheese (optional)
salt

1. Put the water and millet in a small pot. Cover and bring to a boil. Reduce the heat to low and simmer for 20 minutes, until the water is absorbed. Remove from the heat, place the lid askew on top of the pot, and let sit for 5 minutes.

2. Meanwhile, heat a medium pan over medium heat. Lightly coat the pan with oil. Add the shallot, bell pepper, and tempeh. Cook for 4-5 minutes, until the tempeh is just beginning to brown. Remove from the heat.

3. Preheat the oven to 350°F. Place the cooked millet, vegetables, tempeh, walnuts, herbs, and cheese (if using) in

the bowl of a food processor. Pulse until evenly chopped and a slight paste forms. Season with salt to taste.
4. Grease a large baking sheet. Roll the mixture into 1-inch balls, and set on the sheet. Bake for 20 minutes. Flip the balls over and bake for another 20 minutes.

Makes 20-25 "meatballs"

These meatballs are nice with buttered noodles. I like the cheese for an extra boost of flavor, but it's not required.

# Couscous Fig Radicchio Wraps

*Filling*
olive oil for the pot
1 medium shallot, minced
just over 1⅓ cups orange juice
⅔ cup gluten-free brown rice couscous
⅓ cup coarsely chopped dried Mission figs
⅓ cup coarsely chopped almonds
1 bay leaf
½ teaspoon dried parsley
pinch ground cayenne pepper
salt
1 head radicchio lettuce

*Dipping Sauce*
2 tablespoons tahini
2 tablespoons Greek yogurt
2 tablespoons warm water
1 teaspoon apple cider vinegar
1 teaspoon honey
salt

1. For the filling, heat a medium pot over medium heat. Lightly coat the bottom of the pot with oil. Add the shallot and cook 2-3 minutes, until softened.
2. Add the orange juice, couscous, figs, almonds, bay leaf, parsley, cayenne, and a large pinch of salt. Increase the heat to high, cover, and bring to a boil. Reduce the heat

to low and simmer for 13-15 minutes, until the liquid is entirely absorbed.

3. Meanwhile, whisk all of the dipping sauce ingredients together in a small bowl, seasoning to taste with salt.

4. Cut the core out of the head of the radicchio, and slowly pull whole leaves away from the head. Wash and set on towels to dry.

5. Once all of the orange juice is absorbed, stir the couscous to evenly distribute the other ingredients. To serve, spoon approximately ¼ cup of the couscous into a leaf of radicchio. Set the sauce out on the side for dipping or drizzling.

Serves 4

# Fried Rice

2 large eggs
peanut or vegetable oil for the pan
2 small red bell peppers (¾ pound), cut into ½-inch pieces
2 cups shredded cabbage
1 8-ounce can bamboo shoots, drained
4-5 cloves garlic, minced
4 scallions or green onions, diced
1 tablespoon minced ginger
pinch crushed red pepper
2 cups chilled cooked brown jasmine rice
¼ cup sherry, Shaoxing wine, or water
2 tablespoons gluten-free soy sauce or tamari

1. Heat a wok or large pan over high heat. Beat one of the eggs in a bowl. Add about ½ teaspoon of oil to the wok. Add the egg and quickly swirl the wok so the egg makes a thin pancake. Allow to set—this should only take a matter of seconds—and then flip the egg. After a few more seconds remove the egg from the wok and place on a cutting board. Repeat the process with the other egg. Roll each egg into a tube and thinly slice.
2. Add 1 teaspoon of oil to the wok. Add the bell peppers. Fry, stirring occasionally, until lightly seared, around 3 minutes. Set aside in a bowl.

3. Add 1 teaspoon of oil to the wok. Add the cabbage. Fry, stirring occasionally, until lightly seared, around 2 minutes. Set aside in a bowl.

4. Add ½ teaspoon of oil to the wok. Add the bamboo shoots. Fry, stirring occasionally, until lightly seared, around 2-3 minutes. Set aside in a bowl.

5. Add 1 teaspoon of oil to the wok. Add the garlic, scallions, ginger, and crushed red pepper. Fry for 30 seconds, then add in the rice, making sure to break up any clumps. Stir well, and then fry for a few minutes, until the rice is starting to brown.

6. Return the peppers, cabbage, bamboo, and eggs to the wok. Add in the wine or water and soy sauce or tamari. Cook until everything is heated through, around 2 minutes.

Serves 4-6

The rice must be chilled so that it dries out. It's best if it has been refrigerated overnight. If not chilled, the rice steams and gets gloppy. This version is fairly veggie-heavy for fried rice.

# Basil Butter Beans

1 15-ounce can whole peeled tomatoes
olive oil for the pan
1 small carrot (2 ounces), ends trimmed, diced
½ medium yellow onion, diced
3-4 cloves garlic, minced
salt and freshly ground black pepper
2 15-ounce cans butter beans (approximately 3½ cups), drained and rinsed
1½ cups fresh basil, thinly sliced

1. Place the tomatoes and their juice in a medium bowl. Tear the tomatoes into bite-sized pieces.
2. Heat a large pan over medium heat. Lightly coat the pan with oil. Add the carrot and onion and cook until they begin to soften, about 3 minutes. Add the garlic and cook until fragrant, about 30 seconds.
3. Stir in the tomatoes and juices. Add a pinch of salt and a few grinds of pepper. Cook until the tomato juice begins to bubble. Add the beans and cook until they are heated through, 5-10 minutes.
4. Stir in the basil and let it wilt, about 1 minute.

Serves 4

# Desserts

# Rice Pudding

3 cups unsweetened soymilk
½ cup Arborio rice
½ cup sweetened shredded coconut
½ cup packed brown sugar
salt
½ cup dried cherries, roughly chopped

1. Whisk together the milk, rice, coconut, sugar, and a pinch of salt in a medium pot. Set over high heat and bring to a boil. Reduce the heat to medium-low. Simmer, stirring occasionally, until the milk is mostly absorbed, about 35-40 minutes.
2. Add the cherries and cook an additional 10 minutes, until the cherries soften.

Serves 4-6

# Peach Galette

*Crust*
⅔ cup sorghum flour
2 tablespoons brown rice flour
½ cup tapioca starch
2 tablespoons white sugar
½ teaspoon xanthan gum
½ teaspoon salt
8 tablespoons cold butter (1 stick), cut into large chunks
¼ cup cold water

*Filling*
3-4 peaches (1 pound)
1 tablespoon honey
½ teaspoon ground ginger
1 ounce mascarpone cheese (optional)

1. For the crust, whisk together the flours, starch, sugar, xanthan gum, and salt in a medium bowl. Lay out a sheet of plastic wrap nearby. Add the flour mixture and butter to the bowl of a food processor. Pulse until the butter is incorporated but still fairly large in size. Slowly pour the water through the feed tube while pulsing. Stop once the dough looks crumbly and the butter is pea-sized.
2. Turn the mixture out onto the plastic wrap. Gather up the sides of the wrap and press the dough into a ball.

Form into a disk, wrap in the plastic wrap, and refrigerate for 30 minutes.

3. Thinly slice the peaches and place in a medium bowl. Add the honey and ginger, stir well, and let sit.

4. Preheat the oven to 400°F. Line a large baking sheet with parchment paper. Lay out two large overlapping sheets of plastic wrap. Dust the plastic wrap with sorghum flour. Have extra sheets ready to lay on top of the dough.

5. Put the chilled dough on the floured plastic wrap. Sprinkle flour over the top of the dough, and then lay two sheets of plastic wrap over the top. Roll out the dough, stopping to add more flour a few times, until it is a rough circle about ⅛-inch thick. Remove the top sheets of plastic wrap. Hold the rolling pin close to the edge of the dough. Lift the nearest edge of the plastic wrap up and over the rolling pin, so that the dough drapes over the rolling pin. Pull the plastic wrap away from the dough. Transfer the dough to the parchment-lined baking sheet.

6. Distribute the peaches around the dough, leaving one inch around the edges. Avoid transferring the juices from the peaches. Fold the edges of the dough up over the peaches to make a crust. Bake for 45 minutes, until the crust is lightly browned. Remove and let cool. If desired, dot with mascarpone cheese and/or an extra drizzle of honey to serve.

Serves 6-8

I use two sheets of overlapping plastic wrap to ensure I have enough space to roll out the dough. If the dough starts to crack while rolling out, simply lift the plastic wrap and press the two sections together. You can also press little crumbs from around the edges back into the dough.

If you do plan to add mascarpone, it is important to let the galette cool first, otherwise the cheese will melt.

# Chocolate Applesauce Cupcakes

1 cup white sugar
⅓ cup tapioca starch
⅓ cup gluten-free oat flour
⅓ cup sorghum flour
3 tablespoons coconut flour
3 tablespoons cocoa powder
1 teaspoon ground cinnamon
½ teaspoon xanthan gum
¼ teaspoon baking soda
¼ teaspoon salt
½ cup applesauce
2 tablespoons unsweetened soymilk
2 tablespoons light olive oil

1. Preheat the oven to 350°F. Line a 12-cup muffin tin with cupcake liners.
2. In a large mixing bowl, whisk together the sugar, starch, flours, cocoa, cinnamon, xanthan gum, baking soda, and salt.
3. Make a well in the center of the dry ingredients. Stir together the applesauce, milk, and oil in the well, and then mix into the dry ingredients.
4. Spoon the batter into the prepared muffin cups. Bake for 20-25 minutes, until a toothpick inserted in a cupcake comes out clean.

5. Remove the cupcakes from the tin and set on a cooling rack to cool completely.

Makes 12 cupcakes

This batter is very thick. In terms of sweetness, these are right on the border between muffins and cupcakes.

# Blueberry Mango Crisp

*Filling*
1½ cups blueberries
1½ mangos, cut into small chunks (1½ cups)
2 tablespoons white sugar
1 tablespoon freshly squeezed lime juice

*Crisp Topping*
½ cup tapioca starch
¼ cup almond meal
¼ cup sorghum flour
¼ cup white sugar
¼ teaspoon salt
2 tablespoons unsweetened soymilk
2 tablespoons coconut oil

1. Preheat the oven to 375°F.
2. For the filling, stir the blueberries, mangos, sugar, and lime juice together in a large bowl, until the sugar starts to dissolve.
3. In a medium bowl, thoroughly whisk together the starch, almond meal, flour, sugar, and salt. Add the milk and coconut oil and mix until crumbly.
4. Place the filling in an 8×8-inch casserole dish or 9-inch pie plate. Sprinkle the crumble evenly over the top. Bake for 30-35 minutes, until the filling is bubbling and the crisp is starting to brown. Let cool slightly before serving.

Serves 8

Both fresh and frozen fruit work in this recipe, but I think fresh gives a better texture.

# Chocolate Wafer Cookies

¾ cup cocoa powder
⅔ cup sorghum flour
¼ cup millet flour
5 teaspoons cornstarch
½ teaspoon xanthan gum
¼ teaspoon salt
1 cup white sugar
6 tablespoons butter (¾ stick), room temperature
1 large egg
1 teaspoon vanilla extract

1. Thoroughly whisk together the cocoa, flours, starch, xanthan gum, and salt in a medium bowl.
2. In the bowl of a stand mixer, cream the sugar and butter until light and fluffy. Mix in the egg and vanilla until thoroughly incorporated. Add the flour mixture and stir until combined. The dough can be worked with your hands as necessary.
3. Separate the dough into 4 equal-sized balls, then flatten slightly into disks. Wrap each disk separately in plastic wrap and refrigerate for 30 minutes.
4. Preheat the oven to 400°F. Line a baking sheet with parchment paper. Remove one disk, and roll between two sheets of parchment paper, until just under ⅛-inch thick. Cut into 2-inch circles using a cookie or biscuit cutter. Remove excess dough and place cut cookies on

the baking sheet. Bake for 10 minutes. Excess dough can be remolded into a ball, and returned to the refrigerator until ready to reroll. Repeat with the remaining dough until used up.

Makes approximately 60 2-inch cookies

# Coconut Banana Custard Pie

*Crust*
2 cups finely ground chocolate wafer cookie crumbs
(from previous recipe)
4 tablespoons butter (½ stick), melted
salt

*Filling*
1 can full-fat coconut milk (1¾ cups)
⅔ cup white sugar
½ cup unsweetened soymilk
1 teaspoon vanilla extract
3 egg yolks from large eggs
3 medium bananas, cut into ¼-½ inch thick slices
2 tablespoons tapioca starch

1. Preheat the oven to 350°F.
2. For the crust, place the cookie crumbs, butter and a large pinch of salt in a 9-inch pie plate. Stir until a paste forms. Press the crumbs into the pie plate and up the edges. Bake for 10 minutes. Remove and let cool completely before preceding to the next step.
3. For the filling, place the coconut milk, sugar, milk, and vanilla in a medium pot. Beat the egg yolks in a medium bowl. Arrange one layer of banana slices in the pie crust.
4. Set the pot over medium heat and stir until the sugar is dissolved. Once simmering, which should take around 3-4 minutes, spoon some of the heated milk into the egg

yolks while whisking constantly. Whisk in the tapioca starch. Add the egg-tapioca mixture back to the pot, while whisking. The milk should thicken almost immediately. Continue whisking about 30 seconds, and then pour half of the filling over prepared pie crust. Place another layer of bananas over the custard, then top with the remaining filling. Put in the refrigerator to cool completely.

Serves 8-10

This recipe happens quickly, so it is important to have all the ingredients ready before starting.

Since coconut milk is thick, it doesn't bubble like water when simmering. It's more like tomato sauce in that it splatters. Stirring will keep the splattering down.

I have made the crust with store-bought chocolate chunk cookies and found I needed less butter. If you use store-bought cookies, start with 2 tablespoons butter. You want the crumbs to be just wet enough to press into the pie plate.

# Basic Peanut Butter Cookies

½ cup tapioca starch
½ cup sorghum flour
¼ cup millet flour
½ teaspoon baking powder
¼ teaspoon xanthan gum
¼ teaspoon salt
1 cup packed light brown sugar
8 tablespoons butter (1 stick), room temperature
½ cup peanut butter
1 large egg
½ teaspoon vanilla extract

1. Preheat the oven to 350°F. Line baking sheets with parchment paper.
2. Thoroughly whisk together the starch, flours, baking powder, xanthan gum, and salt in a medium bowl.
3. In the bowl of a stand mixer, cream the sugar and butter together. Add the peanut butter, egg, and vanilla and mix until thoroughly incorporated. Add in the flour mixture and mix until well combined.
4. Drop the dough in tablespoon-sized portions onto the baking sheet. Allow some space between the cookies, as they spread. Gently roll each portion into a ball, then slightly flatten.

5. Bake on the center rack for 15 minutes, until just slightly darkened around the edges. Allow to cool completely before serving.

Makes approximately 30 cookies

# Baklava Rolls

½ cup shelled pistachios
¼ cup walnuts
½ teaspoon ground cinnamon
¼ teaspoon ground allspice
1 tablespoon + 1 teaspoon honey
8 16-centimeter circular rice papers
2 tablespoons butter, melted

1. Preheat the oven to 400°F. Place the pistachios and walnuts in the bowl of a food processor and pulse until finely ground.
2. Stir together the nuts, cinnamon, and allspice in a medium bowl. Stir in honey until well combined.
3. Fill a low wide bowl with warm water. Have a flat working surface ready.
4. Dip one rice paper in the water and let soften, 20-30 seconds. Lay out on the work surface. Brush each side with butter. Scoop a tightly-packed tablespoon of the nut mixture. In your hands, form the filling into a cylinder about 3 inches long and place it a couple of inches from one edge of the rice paper. Fold that end over the nuts, and then fold in each side. Roll up and place on a baking sheet. Continue with the remaining ingredients.
5. Bake for 13-15 minutes.

Serves 4

The rolls do not have to be served directly from the oven, but they are most crispy when warm. As they cool the rice paper becomes chewier.

While baking, if the ends of the rolls become very dark or it looks like the paper is starting to crack, remove the rolls from the oven.

# Fudgy Sea Salt Brownies

8 tablespoons butter (1 stick) + more for the casserole dish
3 tablespoons sorghum flour
3 tablespoons tapioca starch
¼ teaspoon salt
8 ounces semi-sweet chocolate, chopped
¾ cup white sugar
2 large eggs
5 ounces dark chocolate and caramel bar
coarse sea salt

1. Preheat the oven to 350°F. Line an 8×8-inch casserole dish with parchment paper and lightly grease. Whisk the flour and starch together in a small bowl.
2. Melt the butter in a medium pot over low heat. Add the salt and chocolate and cook while stirring frequently, until the chocolate is melted. Immediately remove from the heat.
3. Pour the chocolate mixture into a large bowl or the bowl of a stand mixer with whisk attachment. Whisk in the sugar. Whisk in the eggs, one at a time. Whisk in the flour blend.
4. Pour half of the batter into the prepared casserole dish. Break or chop the chocolate bar and layer the pieces with a sprinkle of coarse sea salt over the batter. Pour the remaining batter on top and smooth to the edges.

5. Bake for 30 minutes, until the middle is just set. Let cool before cutting.

Makes 16 brownies

# Stuffed Poached Pears

1 750-ml bottle + 2 cups dry red wine
¾ cup white sugar + 2 tablespoons, divided
1-2 small cinnamon sticks
¼ teaspoon whole cloves
2 tablespoons lemon juice
4 ripe Anjou pears (2 pounds)
2-4 ounces mascarpone cheese

1. Place the wine, ¾ cup sugar, cinnamon, and cloves in a medium pot. Set over medium-high heat.
2. Meanwhile, fill a large bowl with cold water and stir in the lemon juice. Core the pears from the bottom. Slice a little off the bottom end so that the pear can stand up, then peel. Place each pear in the lemon water after peeling to keep from browning.
3. Once the wine mixture is boiling, reduce the heat to low and add the pears. Simmer the pears until soft, 30-45 minutes, making sure to turn them periodically if they're not entirely covered by the wine mixture.
4. Remove the pears from the pot and set aside to cool. Remove the cloves and cinnamon sticks. Discard (or reserve***) all but 1 cup of the wine. Return the 1 cup of wine to the pot and add the remaining 2 tablespoons of sugar. Set over medium-high heat. Let the wine mixture boil until it's reduced by half, around 15 minutes. Remove from the heat and let cool.

5. Once the pears are at room temperature, stuff each with mascarpone. To serve, place a pear in the middle of a small plate and spoon the wine syrup over the top. Repeat with remaining pears and syrup.

Serves 4

The longer the pears cook, the more color they take on. Pears can be made a day ahead of time and allowed to soak, refrigerated, in the wine.

Be sure to let the pears cool before stuffing with the cheese, otherwise the cheese melts and drips out of the bottom.

***The extra wine can be served as mulled wine.

# Amaretto Cake

## Frosting
3 cups whipping cream
6 ounces semi-sweet chocolate, roughly chopped
¼ cup powdered sugar

## Cake
½ cup vegetable oil + more for the pans
1½ cups white sugar, divided
1 cup tapioca starch
½ cup millet flour
½ cup white rice flour
¼ cup sorghum flour
1½ teaspoons xanthan gum
1 teaspoon baking powder
½ teaspoon salt
4 large eggs, separated
½ cup unsweetened soymilk
1½ teaspoons vanilla extract
½ cup Amaretto liqueur, divided

1. For the frosting, place the whipping cream and chocolate in a medium pot. Set over medium heat. Cook, whisking lightly, until the chocolate is just melted, 6-8 minutes. Refrigerate until completely chilled, at least 2-3 hours.
2. For the cake, preheat the oven to 350°F. Grease the bottom of two 10-inch cake pans.

3. Whisk 1 cup sugar with the starch, flours, xanthan gum, baking powder, and salt in a large bowl.

4. Place the egg whites and remaining ½ cup sugar in the bowl of a stand mixer with whisk attachment. Beat over medium speed, until soft peaks form.

5. Meanwhile, lightly whisk together the egg yolks, milk, vegetable oil, and vanilla in a medium bowl. Pour into the dry mixture and stir until combined. The batter will be very stiff.

6. Fold one-third of the egg whites into the batter, until thoroughly incorporated. Fold in the remaining egg whites. Spoon the batter evenly between the cake pans and smooth it to the edges of the pans.

7. Bake for 25-30 minutes, until the cake is light golden-brown on the top and springs back when touched. Set upside-down on cooling racks and let cool completely.

8. When ready to assemble, place the chocolate whipping cream in the bowl of a stand mixer with whisk attachment. Beat over medium speed. Slowly whip in the powdered sugar until clear streaks that keep their shape form. If the mixture starts to look grainy, stop mixing.

9. Place one layer of cake on a serving platter. Poke all over with a toothpick. Brush half of the Amaretto onto the cake. Spread a layer of frosting on top. Poke holes in the second cake and set it on top of the first layer. Brush the remaining Amaretto on the cake. Frost the top and sides of the cake.

Serves 8-10

Be gentle folding the egg whites into the cake batter. Also, take your time, as it can take a while to get them completely incorporated.

The chocolate whipped cream can be chilled for longer. It can be useful to chill the bowl and beaters in the freezer for 15 minutes before making the frosting. The recipe makes plenty of frosting, so be generous between layers and on the sides.

## Acknowledgements:

Special thanks go to Alisa Fleming for editing what was a giant mess. The readers have you to thank for ordered ingredients and instructions that actually make sense.

Thanks also go to Victoria Valentine who, with very little direction, produced a beautiful cover I'm proud to show to the world.

## About the Author:

Kalinda Piper is the author of the popular blog Wheat-FreeMeatFree.com, which currently has more than 7,000 email subscribers. She lives in Manitou Springs, Colorado, where she enjoys rock climbing and hiking with her husband. She still isn't allowed to wield a chef's knife in her parents' kitchen.

# Index

Made in the USA
Lexington, KY
15 November 2014